This Place on Earth 2001

Other Northwest Environment Watch Titles

State of the Northwest, revised 2000 edition

Seven Wonders:
Everyday Things for a Healthier Planet

Green-Collar Jobs

Tax Shift

Over Our Heads:
A Local Look at Global Climate

Misplaced Blame:
The Real Roots of Population Growth

Stuff: The Secret Lives of Everyday Things

This Place on Earth:
Home and the Practice of Permanence

The Car and the City

Hazardous Handouts:
Taxpayer Subsidies to Environmental Degradation

State of the Northwest

This Place on Earth 2001

Guide to a Sustainable Northwest

NORTHWEST ENVIRONMENT WATCH ◆ SEATTLE

NORTHWEST ENVIRONMENT WATCH IS AN INDEPENDENT, not-for-profit research and communication center in Seattle, Washington, with an affiliated charitable organization, NEW BC, in Victoria, British Columbia. Their joint mission: to foster a sustainable economy and way of life throughout the Pacific Northwest—the biological region stretching from southern Alaska to northern California and from the Pacific Ocean to the crest of the Rockies.

Library of Congress Catalog Card Number: 2001087926
ISBN 1-886093-11-3

Design and cover illustration: Cathy Schwartz
Interior illustration: Yu-Ming Zhu
Editing and composition: Ellen W. Chu
Proofreading: Sherri Schultz

Printed by Alpha One Corporation, Redmond, Washington, with vegetable-based ink on recycled paper. Text: 100 percent postconsumer waste, bleached with hydrogen peroxide. Cover: 50 percent preconsumer waste, bleached with hydrogen peroxide.

Northwest Environment Watch is a 501(c)(3) tax-exempt organization. To order Northwest Environment Watch titles or to become a member, please contact us:

Northwest Environment Watch
1402 Third Avenue, Suite 500
Seattle, WA 98101-2130 USA
(206) 447-1880; fax (206) 447-2270
new@northwestwatch.org; www.northwestwatch.org

NEW BC
P.O. Box 301, 2250 Oak Bay Avenue
Victoria, BC
V8R 1G5 Canada
(250) 595-0577; fax (250) 595-0575
info@newbc.org; www.newbc.org

C O N T E N T S

P R E F A C E

As this book goes to press in March 2001, faulty deregulation of California's electricity market, combined with record-low water levels in hydropower reservoirs, has dimmed lights in the Golden State, tightened power supplies throughout the West, and darkened prospects for the Northwest's endangered salmon.

This crisis is an object lesson in how much the Northwest depends on nature. It's also a lesson in how wrong things go when societies fail to align incentives sent by their institutions with objectives shared by their people. Markets convey especially potent signals, coordinating the actions of millions of people through the power of the pocketbook. They are awesomely efficient at what they do, and quick to wreak havoc when they aren't aligned with public goals—such as providing electricity or protecting salmon—as California's experience demonstrates.

This Place on Earth 2001 catalogs high-leverage ways, many of them using markets, to steer the Northwest toward a sustainable economy and way of life—a Northwest that honors its dependence on nature. These catalytic reforms prompt dramatic leaps, not plodding steps, toward the goal. They are what the region can do to prevent future crises like the one spreading from California.

This volume is also the premiere edition of a new annual book series from Northwest Environment Watch (NEW). *This Place on Earth 2001* addresses the first of two questions organizing the series: What are the most critical things to do for reconciling economy and environment in the Northwest? Each year, helped by many northwesterners, NEW will improve on the previous year's answers and ultimately identify the handful of reforms that will unleash the most progress.

Early next year, the second volume, *This Place on Earth 2002*, will turn to NEW's second question: How is the Northwest doing at reconciling itself with nature? By identifying a small set of indicators, NEW will design—again helped by many northwesterners—an index of true progress for the region. Conceived as an alternative to conventional measures of progress, such as gross national product, the final index will be at least two years in the making.

The series title comes from NEW's award-winning 1996 book, *This Place on Earth: Home and the Practice of Permanence*. That book articulated a vision; this book and its successors will add a pragmatic strategy for achieving the vision—and a way to track progress along the way.

Metric equivalents are given for the convenience of Canadian readers; dollars are US dollars and tons are short tons unless noted otherwise.

T H I S P L A C E

SPREADING ACROSS BRITISH COLUMBIA, IDAHO, Washington, Oregon, and adjoining parts of Alaska, Montana, and California, the Pacific Northwest is home to 15.5 million people, along with diminished but still impressive numbers of salmon, eagles, grizzly bears, killer whales, and wolves. It boasts an economy—concentrated along Interstate 5 and its Canadian equivalent, Route 99—that generates more than $400 billion worth of goods and services each year, enough to make northwesterners some of the richest people ever.[1]

Long united by similar indigenous cultures, this region, often called "Cascadia," was once briefly a single political unit—the Oregon Territory—shared by several nations. It remains one place shared by different political jurisdictions, now with a dawning sense of itself: a place bound by salmon and rivers, snowcapped mountains and towering forests.[2]

The Northwest has traditions of innovation in the public and private sectors; a well-educated populace; and, above all, a commitment to conservation. Indeed, the environment is, in many ways, the Northwest's defining issue. This biological region retains a larger share of its ecosystems intact than perhaps any other part of the industrial world. It has helped set the conservation agenda for the continent—with the first bottle bills and urban growth management laws in the 1970s; trend-setting energy conservation and curbside recycling efforts in the 1980s; old-growth forest protection in the 1990s; and, now, the first endangered species listings to affect major cities.[3]

But there's a broader environmental challenge to which the Northwest is just beginning to rise—not conservation but sustainability: gradually but fundamentally realigning the human enterprise so that both economies and their supporting ecosystems can thrive. Daunting, complex, systemic, seemingly quixotic, sustainability is nonetheless more attainable here than anywhere else on this continent.

A I K I D O P O L I T I C S

Aikido is the subtlest of martial arts: students never meet their opponents' force head on; rather, they deflect it. With precise timing and dancelike movements—graceful gestures that apply redirecting pressure to strategic points of an opponent's anatomy—students use their antagonists' own momentum to throw or pin them.

Many of aikido's techniques grew out of jujitsu, the ancient Japanese samurai's "gentle art" of hand-to-hand combat. Jujitsu techniques allow practitioners to overcome opponents of greater size and strength. As used by the samurai, jujitsu was, if brutally effective, anything but gentle. In contrast, aikido—founded in 1942 by Japanese military hero Morihei Ueshiba after a lifetime of developing its techniques—strives not to harm but to protect opponents, to turn their destructive aims to constructive ends. Aikido means "way of harmony" or, literally, "way to harmonize with nature's energy."[4]

LIKE THE EASTERLY AND WESTERLY WINDS THAT HOWL up and down the Columbia Gorge, controversy has whipsawed the Northwest since the new millennium began: the Internet bubble burst, gasoline prices surged, elections went haywire, electricity went south, the economy flirted with recession, an earthquake shook Puget Sound. And controversy is as impossible to ignore as icy gorge winds when they sweep the streets of Portland.

But beneath the gusts of controversy that grabs headlines, deeper forces are shaping the Northwest. In the gorge, while air currents hold the attention of sailboarders and power generators (who are erecting the largest wind-electric plant in the world there), the Columbia itself—the biggest Pacific-bound river in the Americas—presses steadily westward. Its current, deep and slow beneath the wind-driven waves, gnaws down the Cascades as it has for millions of years.[5]

In the Northwest this past year, most of the changes felt in homes, businesses, and communities have flowed not from the headlines but from the region's deeper, slower current: the enormous scale—and growth—of the human enterprise. Make no mistake: elections, energy crises, Wall Street squalls, and earthquakes alter life in the Northwest, but their effects are like the wind atop the river.

Even with a tempering economy, the human presence in the Northwest expanded impressively in 2000:

- The cash value of all goods and services sold in British Columbia, Idaho, Oregon, and Washington grew by about $15 billion—an increase larger than the entire economy of Guatemala. (If the Northwest were an independent country, its economy would now be the 15th largest in the world, ahead of Mexico's and Russia's. In per capita purchasing power, the Northwest would trail only the United States.)[6]

- The human population of the Northwest rose by 250,000, a slightly smaller increase than during many recent years but more than the number of travelers on the Oregon Trail in all the decades it brought pioneers to the region. (The Northwest's population surpassed that of the Netherlands during 2000. Were the Northwest an independent nation, it would be the 57th most populous.)[7]

- The number of households—as important as sheer population size because households are the basic units of consumption for environmentally critical goods such as homes, vehicles, appliances, and energy—swelled by an estimated 100,000. The number of houses and apartments grew by approximately the same amount.[8]

- The region's fleet of motor vehicles increased by more than 200,000, with truck sales outpacing car sales. If current trends continue, trucks will outnumber cars in the region in 2005.[9]

Growth brought benefits: it raised families' incomes, including those of poor northwesterners; it expanded the Northwest's diversity of economic and cultural offerings; and it made the region's cities more cosmopolitan. It also imposed costs, including rising real estate prices, crowded parks, and congested highways. Above all, growth augmented the scale of human actions that erode ecosystems. That scale was already staggering: on average last year, through the global economy, the 15.5 million northwesterners consumed each day their body weight in natural resources—resources extracted from farms, fisheries, forests, mines, and grasslands. Each day, they also consumed more than 1,000 gallons (3,785 liters) of water apiece (Idahoans pumped more water per person than the citizens of any nation in the world) and emitted nearly their body weight in climate-changing air pollutants.[10]

As a consequence of northwesterners' everyday actions, during 2000, their region:

- Paved or otherwise developed more than 100 square miles (260 square kilometers) of rural land.[11]
- Clearcut about 700 square miles (1,800 square kilometers) of previously unlogged forest.[12]
- Consumed more than 5 trillion gallons (19 trillion liters) of water, mostly for irrigation.[13]
- Watched as the number of orcas in Puget Sound and Georgia Strait dwindled, their bodies containing higher concentrations of toxic polychlorinated biphenyls (PCBs) than any other mammals in the world.[14]
- Struggled with little success to reverse the decline of endangered wild salmon runs in much of the region, even as more than 130 other species on official lists of endangered species faced peril and perhaps ten times as many, not listed officially, also fared poorly.[15]
- Released about 5.5 million tons of regulated pollutants into the air, water, and land.[16]
- Burned enough gasoline and other fossil fuels to inject 200 million tons of climate-changing carbon dioxide into the atmosphere.[17]

For this generation of northwesterners, the defining challenge is to redirect the deep current of growth in ways that enable its benefits to accrue while deflecting its costs. More simply stated, our calling is to achieve sustainability: an economy and way of life in which both people and nature flourish, a culture that can last.

This mission is not unique to this place; it is a global goal, defined by the great paradox of recent history: our success is undermining itself. We are the most successful species on likely the only planet in the Milky Way that's home to complex animal life. We have adapted to virtually all terrestrial habitats and generated more living matter, or protoplasm, simultaneously than any other single species ever. In the last 300 years, we have increased our average body size by half; doubled our average lifespan; multiplied our population tenfold; and increased our use of water, soils, and other resources many hundredfold. But this remarkable success has jeopardized much of Earth's rich living sphere, destabilizing the global climate, dooming species to extinction at a rate exceeding one per hour, and lacing the world's food webs with synthetic chemicals.[18]

Reconciling economy and ecology in the Northwest would be globally significant, inspiring other regions to do the same. But sustainability entails dramatic change. A case in point: If humanity is to stabilize global climate, it must reduce its emissions of greenhouse gases by 60 percent or more. Population growth and increased fuel consumption in developing countries are inevitable, so, to do their share in stabilizing the climate, northwesterners must trim their collective emissions of greenhouse gases by a disproportionate amount. Reasonable assumptions lead to the target of an 80 or 90 percent reduction within the span of a century at most. What's more, northwesterners will have to achieve these reductions in the face of growing population and income.[19]

Fortunately, such change has precedents. Humans are amazingly adaptable. Our society remakes itself constantly as new laws, technologies, and demographic and cultural forces shift behavior and change the humanmade infrastructure. The Northwest converted from the horse to the car in less than 50 years and is in the midst of a similar conversion to a society based on the microchip.[20]

Unquestionably, in the next century the region will change profoundly, and northwesterners can seize the opportunity to alter their trajectory. The audacious energy that dammed and diverts the Columbia and other Northwest rivers can steer the current of growth toward ecological reconciliation. Even small deflections can push the current in radically different directions. The Northwest reduced its per capita emissions of carbon dioxide by 3.1 percent a year between 1973 and 1983, when energy was even more expensive than in this past year. Matching that pace would reduce emissions two-thirds by 2100, even if the population grew as fast as it did during the second half of the twentieth century. If the region's population grew at half that rate during the twenty-first century, greenhouse gas emissions would decline by almost 90 percent by 2100. And if either population stabilized or per-person emissions of greenhouse gases declined by 4 percent annually, the Northwest would approach an 80 percent reduction in just 50 years.[21]

Still, a 3 or 4 percent annual rate of change is swift, a speed the Northwest can achieve only if it finds the strategic points where a little reverse engineering—a weir or culvert here, diking or breaching there—will shift the current. The existing flow streams from innumerable discrete actions. Northwesterners, to cite three examples, made tens of billions of purchases last year, drove vehicles on 10 billion trips, and—speaking of root causes of growth—had sex perhaps 180 million times.[22]

Achieving sustainability is impossible unless the North-west can influence actions by the millions and billions, not merely by the hundreds or thousands. Fortunately, the region's tax codes, government budgets, land-use plans, insurance regulations, medical rules, and environmental standards form the channels through which the human enterprise flows. And these channels are replete with points where deflection, art-fully applied, can turn the Northwest's demographic, eco-nomic, and social current in new directions.

For example, in 1997 the US federal government allowed Americans to keep, free from income tax, profits from sales of their homes. Previously, homeowners had to apply the proceeds toward the purchase of another home within two years until they retired, when they were allowed one chance to "cash out" their home free of tax. This obscure new policy is factoring into the thinking of millions of people, encourag-ing many empty-nesters to trade down to smaller homes, of-ten closer to the center of town, thus slowing suburban sprawl. Slowing sprawl protects rural lands and the ecosystems there. It also makes the urban human habitat more compact, which makes driving less necessary; less car travel in turn improves local air quality, diminishes crash deaths, and even helps sta-bilize the global climate. Now, that's deflection.[23]

Deflection is a routine practice in hydrology and optics, but its fullest human use may be in the martial art of aikido. And aikido, as Amory and Hunter Lovins of the Rocky Moun-tain Institute have long suggested, forms a nearly perfect meta-phor for the political approach most appropriate to the challenge of sustainability. Aikido politics is a respectful, patient dance that redirects the momentum of business as usual toward positive ends.[24]

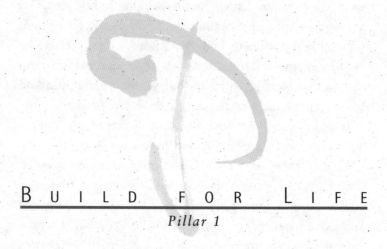

B U I L D   F O R   L I F E
Pillar 1

Aikido rests on six clusters of techniques, called pillars. The first pillar, the "four-directions throw," requires continual practice but is often the first technique taught to beginners. In its several variants, the four-directions throw makes full and efficient use of space to draw the opponent to the center of a tightening spiral.

    Lesson: *An attacker swings at your temple. Quickly back out of reach and grab his oncoming fist. As his fist passes your head, push it onward in the direction it was already going, continuing the attacker's momentum. Still guiding his fist, circle the attacker quickly and direct his fist in a closing spiral, like a tetherball wrapping itself to the pole. His body rotates out of balance as the momentum of his lunge pushes him toward where you used to be, while you twirl him around. He ends up on the ground in the very center of the spiral.*[25]

THE ESSENCE OF AIKIDO'S FIRST PILLAR—THE FOUR-directions throw—is to use space wisely, draw an attack off-balance, and send the momentum spinning in on itself. In the Northwest, the force fragmenting, paving, clearing, and depleting ecosystems comes from the cumulative impact of northwesterners' everyday choices—made rationally and in good faith. Northwesterners want safe, friendly neighborhoods to live in; convenient access to shops and services; the opportunity to play in beautiful, unspoiled places; and the freedom to turn hard work into financial security. Timely pressure applied in the right places can send this momentum spinning inward, yielding compact, livable cities that provide for human needs while leaving intact open spaces where wild nature can thrive.

After long years of public dialogue about growth and development, Northwest communities increasingly subscribe to the same vision of the future: Most population growth would concentrate in central cities and in satellite hubs, not spill into undifferentiated sprawl. Downtowns would again be ringed by dense middle-class neighborhoods, with low-income and high-income housing mixed throughout, not in pockets. Streets would function well not only for cars but also for pedestrians, cyclists, and buses. Transit would knit cities together internally and connect seamlessly to train stations and airports. Urban streams, freed from the culverts into which engineers put them decades ago, would meander through restored green spaces—urban wildlife refuges that could double as parks and playing fields. Cities would have crisp edges beyond which ecologically sound farms, forests, and open spaces would stretch. And wildlands, off limits to human development, would provide safe havens—some small refuges, some vast wildernesses—for the living nature the Northwest depends on.

To realize this vision, thousands of northwesterners are making their region a laboratory for the reinvention of humans in place. Knowing that every area rebuilds itself continually over the decades, they are practicing the four-directions throw vigilantly, attempting to recenter their communities and make wise use of space. Revitalization, they are finding, comes in small steps, and those steps have immediate benefits. Block by block, zoning hearing by zoning hearing, forest district by forest district, they are fashioning a living Northwest.

1. GROW CITIES UP, NOT OUT

Motor vehicles are now arguably nature's principal antagonist in the Northwest, and—despite popular perceptions to the contrary—the real alternative to cars is not better transit; it's compact neighborhoods. That's the lesson of rigorous research on driving patterns in cities worldwide. As population density rises, especially as it exceeds two broad thresholds, driving wanes. So rezoning close-in neighborhoods for larger populations, while holding growth boundaries tight on the periphery, will pull whatever growth is inevitable for the Northwest into the center of the region's cities.[26]

Low-density districts, including nine-tenths of greater Portland and greater Seattle and half of greater Vancouver— most of what developers have built since World War II—leave their residents dependent on autos for virtually all trips. But at more than 12 people per acre (4,047 square meters), in medium-density zones such as the older in-city neighborhoods of Seattle and Portland and most of the city of Vancouver, enough riders make regular buses cost-effective. Reliable transit, in turn, frees households from needing as many cars.[27]

Scores of Northwest neighborhoods comprising single-family homes have populations within striking range of medium density. Loosening the restrictions preventing homeowners from renting out accessory apartments—"granny flats" or "mother-in-law apartments"—would throw many neighborhoods across this first threshold. One or two accessory apartments per block would often suffice, even while they enhanced the supply of affordable housing.

Crossing the second threshold, from medium- to high-density areas at roughly 40 people per acre, brings destinations close enough that bicycling and foot travel flourish, people drive two-thirds less than in low-density districts, and as many as one-third of households do not own a car at all. Even affluent residents of high-density areas—think of Seattle's Belltown and First Hill or the booming high-rise neighborhoods around downtown Vancouver—drive less, and ride the bus more, than low-income residents of the suburban periphery. Transit thrives at high densities. In Vancouver's West End, buses run frequently enough—roughly once every seven minutes—that no one needs a schedule. And because those buses are usually full, most turn a profit.[28]

Vancouver's proliferating condominium towers remain the Northwest's most visible urban renaissance and the region's shining example for building "walking zones" at a city's center. Portland and Seattle too have experienced vigorous growth in downtown living in recent years, and smaller cities such as Bend, Boise, and Spokane have followed suit.

Living in compact neighborhoods, especially high-rises, is not for everyone, but most new downtown buildings fill fast.

Market research in greater Seattle shows that although three-fourths of people prefer detached houses to higher-density options, most people care more about the quality of the neighborhood and owning their own home than about housing type. In the right circumstances, more than 90 percent would trade low-density living for medium- or high-density neighborhoods: some would move into high-rises, others into low-rises, townhouses, or detached houses on small lots.[29]

In all the region's cities, planners can spin growth inward through zoning changes that redirect the thrust of sprawl toward vibrant urban cores where people can both live and work. They can hold the line on suburban expansion while encouraging downtown development.

2. DESIGN CITIES FOR WALKING AND BICYCLING

If practiced continually, another four-directions throw can unleash the potential for walking and bicycling as full complements to the automobile. Applying pressure to the leverage points of community design—the mixture of land uses (homes, shops, and workplaces) and the arrangement of buildings, streets, and sidewalks—can make heels and skinny wheels attractive transportation options.

Choices about zoning and urban form can create, or destroy, pedestrian havens. Small city blocks and narrow lots make walking more interesting by creating an intimate ambience for foot travelers, for instance, and a traditional street grid provides better human-powered—and motorized—traffic flow than the sprawl model of cul-de-sacs, feeder roads, connector roads, and highways. Likewise, closely interlacing commercial and residential streets and blending these uses in the same blocks and buildings bring destinations within walking range: allowing apartments above stores, for example, would return to favor what was for generations the main form of affordable housing in Northwest towns. Likewise, replicating throughout the Northwest greater Portland's requirement that all new commercial buildings be close to the street, as in traditional downtowns, would boost walking. In Portland, such neighborhoods induce 15 percent less driving per person than average.[30]

The design of streetscapes is another chance for a four-directions throw. Completing the infrastructure for human-powered travel—sidewalks and bike routes—invites people out of their cars. Fully one-third of Seattle's city streets lack sidewalks, and most of the region's suburbs are even less well provided. Across the region, furthermore, many sidewalks are too narrow or lack the planting strip and street trees that shield pedestrians from moving cars. If anything, the infra-structure for bicycling is worse. No Northwest city has better than a rudimentary cycling network, and the most continuous networks of bike lanes are in smaller cities such as Bend, Eugene, and Victoria. The potential is huge. Upward of a quarter of all car trips in the United States are less than a mile long, and cities that build good routes typically see a tripling of bike travel.[31]

Finally, slowing cars by narrowing streets and installing speed bumps and traffic circles can increase human-powered travel on a street by 10 percent or more. Seattle, the region's leader in traffic calming, has reduced auto accidents by 95 percent at the thousands of intersections it has re-engineered since the 1970s. The next step there, as elsewhere in the region, is to extend traffic calming to larger roads, following the lead of Amsterdam and Tokyo.[32]

3. MAKE BEST TRANSPORTATION BUYS FIRST

One transportation reform that would help spin urban growth inward is the application of least-cost planning, an arcane decision-making technique that's already required by an unenforced law, at least in Washington. Developed a quarter century ago, mostly by northwestern electric-utility planners, least-cost planning is common sense rigorously applied. For electricity, it involves cataloging every way to supply or conserve power, pricing each option (including long-term, social, and environmental costs), publicizing the results, and buying the best options first.[33]

Before the rise of least-cost planning, energy investments poured into massive new power plants, including nuclear stations. After the Northwest Power Planning Council in Portland applied least-cost planning to the regional power market in the early 1980s, however, the Northwest essentially stopped building large power plants. Instead, it invested in conservation, saved billions of dollars for ratepayers, cut growth in annual electricity use from almost 4 percent in the 1970s to about 1.5 percent since, and made the Northwest a world energy leader. Unfortunately, in the mid-1990s, low energy prices and the expectation of utility deregulation led to drastic cuts in conservation investment in the region, as in California, and power demand edged up on supply, helping to create the electricity crisis of early 2001.[34]

The Northwest's transportation sector is now what the energy field was in the 1970s—a tangle to which authorities have responded with ambitious proposals, this time for road expansions and rail transit lines. Again, least-cost planning might find better opportunities. A study of options for greater Seattle concluded that these proposals actually constituted the worst deals. The best buys involved expanding the net-work of transit and carpool lanes, mainly by rededicating freeway lanes; subsidizing carpools; distributing free bus passes; building more bike routes; and deploying more vanpools. Most of these options share the ability to make fuller use of existing space: roads already built and empty seats in vehicles already rolling.[35]

In Curitiba, Brazil, and elsewhere, dedicated bus lanes, "smart" traffic signals that turn green for transit vehicles (greater Portland installed 40 during 2000), and curbside fare collection have worked as well as a rail transit system for a fraction of the cost. Eugene is planning such a bus–rapid tran-sit system, and Seattle has announced plans for bus-only lanes in two corridors. Also winners in least-cost planning, vanpool programs provide vans and match drivers with neighbors whose commutes are similar. The program in King County, Washington, is one of the best on the continent.[36]

Another promising transportation reform is taxi deregu-lation. Early in the automotive age, Model T drivers picked up riders at streetcar stops for a nickel a ride. Before street-car companies convinced cities to ban such private part-time "jitneys" in favor of regulated taxis, this informal pay-carpool system moved some 50,000 riders a day in Seattle. On North-west roads, the typical vehicle now holds a driver and four empty seats, and numerous cars are going the same places at the same times. Information technologies create a chance to slash this previously unavoidable redundancy. A Beaverton, Oregon–based consortium is developing a smart jitney sys-tem—a real-time ride-matching system that relies on handheld computers, a database of registered users, electronic payment, and a dispatching computer.[37]

The essence of least-cost planning, however, is not any of these particular options; it is the discipline of choosing the best combination of investments—the best aikido moves.

4. "PROTECT THE BEST . . .

Humans have radically altered Northwest ecosystems, but the region still possesses many of its wild genes, native communities, and natural processes. Blessed with this wealth, northwesterners retain the means to weave into nature's fabric a durable human economy. Just as urban planners can spin the momentum of human development back toward city centers, others can use aikido to protect the region's unique communities and intact landscapes; they can safeguard the region's ecological options for generations to come.[38]

Among the Northwest's best natural strongholds are its vast wild spaces, which retain the ecological integrity vital to the region's prosperity and quality of life. Roadless forests and watersheds offer sanctuary for salmon and Sitka spruce; for keystone predators like grizzly bears, whose presence structures entire food webs; and for an invisible foundation of fungi and microorganisms. They also sustain the ancient regenerating rhythms of fire and flood and provide humans with benefits ranging from clean water and moderate climates to crop pollination and recreation. In Washington and Oregon alone, studies estimate the dollar value of forest ecosystem services at $21 million annually; the value of such services in US national forests now surpasses that of timber.[39]

Marine reserves are no less vital; keeping certain areas of ocean off limits to human activity enhances the abundance and diversity of marine life not only within reserve boundaries but in surrounding waters as well. Gulf of Maine

scallop fishers, for example, benefit from high catches along
the edges of closed reserves, as young shellfish move outward and replenish harvested waters.[40]

Through public and private initiatives, the Northwest can
expand its share of wildness. This share is already growing,
though parks and monuments still concentrate in scenic and
relatively barren alpine zones. Between 1991 and 2000, British Columbia doubled its protected lands, safeguarding 14
million acres (5.7 million hectares)—an area one-third the
size of Washington. As 2001 began, the White House had
designated close to a quarter million acres (100,000 hectares) of public land in Washington and Oregon as national
monuments and ordered an end to road building and logging
on all roadless tracts of federal land. Scheduled to take effect
by the middle of 2001, the roadless area order will protect
almost 26 million acres (10.5 million hectares) in the Northwest, including nearly 10 million acres (4 million hectares) in
the Tongass National Forest. In eastern Washington, private
donations halted logging on roadless tracts of the Loomis
Forest, and BC created an adjacent provincial park, completing the largest contiguous body of protected lands along
the 4,000-mile (6,436-kilometer) US-Canada boundary. All
told, 16 percent of the region's land is off limits to industry.[41]

Marine protected areas are still scarce. The Olympic Coast
National Marine Sanctuary covers just 2 million acres
(809,000 hectares) of ocean off the Olympic Peninsula, and
BC and the Canadian federal government are planning to
have a system of marine protected areas in place by 2010.
None of these areas will be entirely off limits, however.[42]

Outside of intact wildlands, choosing habitats carefully,
reconnecting fragmented patches, and keeping whole water-

sheds off limits would also protect the "best." Across Oregon, for example, biologists have identified healthy watersheds that are key to retaining the state's aquatic diversity, and they have proposed a salmon-centered "anchor habitat" strategy for its western forests. Because 80 percent of salmon use 18 percent of the available habitat, this plan—which calls for protecting steep slopes; large trees, especially along stream banks; and the reaches and deep pools where salmon concentrate, spawn, and rear—does not set aside large areas but fosters coexistence of humans and fish. Working with the US Forest Service in Washington, the privately funded Cascades Conservation Partnership aims to purchase 75,000 forested acres (30,000 hectares) in the central Cascades to consolidate the checker-board patches once owned by the railroads. And in the Willapa Hills, the Nature Conservancy has set its sights on purchasing an entire 5,000-acre (2,000-hectare) watershed, remarkable for its healthy estuary and its remaining lowland old-growth trees. If the Conservancy succeeds, Ellsworth Creek will be the only wholly protected coastal watershed between Canada and central Oregon.[43]

5. ". . . RESTORE THE REST"

Aikido politics would have northwesterners spinning the momentum for conservation inward from scenic rock and ice to the low-elevation forests, productive lowlands, flood-plains, wetlands, and estuaries surrounding the places where most people live. The monetary value of services provided by these ecosystems is considerable, perhaps as high as $15–30 billion in just Washington and Oregon. Taking advantage of these services—the way Seattle does by barring access to the wooded watershed of the Cedar River, which supplies the city's water—the Northwest can retain healthy landscapes, restore degraded ones, and save money as well.[44]

In suburbs ringing Northwest cities, development can align with natural dynamics while citizens help restore woods and streams. To help protect still-healthy salmon streams in Olympia, Washington, for example, planners rewrote the subdivision rules for the quickly growing and ecologically rich Green Cove Creek basin. The plan shrinks the paved area by narrowing streets, enlarging lot size, and retaining native vegetation. As a result, rainwater soaks into the ground rather than running off into pipes, reducing the need for expensive storm sewers and recharging groundwater sources. In a wooded suburban pocket east of Seattle, the Denny Creek Neighborhood Alliance is working with county officials to protect large trees, replant native streamside vegetation, and restore coho salmon to the creek.[45]

Following nature's lead in the forests and grasslands surrounding population centers would spare the Northwest the future heat and angry debate kindled by wildfire seasons such as the summer of 2000. The fires raged fiercest in managed forests and woodlands backed up against development, where a century and a half of fire suppression and timber cutting had removed the largest trees and left a buildup of flammable small trees and brush. Big old-growth forests in roadless areas did not burn. By thinning small trees, letting some lands burn, and allowing woods to regenerate and grow old, land managers would restore the forests' health and their ability to provide the goods and services northwesterners need.[46]

On Northwest floodplains, restoring natural cycles would bring similar benefits. Consider one particular mile along northeastern Oregon's John Day River. Following the advice of agricultural agencies in the 1970s, George Stubblefield removed fences on his ranch and opened his riverbank to cattle while the agencies "cleaned" the river of woody debris and stripped the shore of "thirsty" trees. The riverbanks eroded; the Army Corps of Engineers straightened the channel and built levees against flooding. Cold, clear water and fish like salmon and trout gave way to warm, muddy water and fish like catfish and bass. Appalled by the change, Stubblefield rebuilt his fences. No longer chewed or trampled, young trees and grasses regrew, slowing the river during high water and filtering enough fine silts to rebuild the banks. Erosion reversed, and complex habitats returned as the river sculpted its own meandering path. When devastating floods roared through Oregon in 1991 and 1995, they slowed and nourished Stubblefield's mile of stream, even as they cut away at his neighbor's shrinking pastures.[47]

R E D I R E C T   M A R K E T S

Pillar 2

"If your partner pulls, let him pull," said aikido founder Morihei, "but become one with that pull." By blending with or entering the attack, the aikido practitioner redirects it. This technique, the "entering throw," is aikido's second pillar and perhaps its quintessential move. It requires placing oneself inside the "danger radius" of an attack by stepping in close to the assailant, leaving her no target and gaining control of her balance. Like a Frisbee caught on a fingertip, spun, and then sent onward with a flip of the wrist, the entering throw follows a contracting and expanding spiral that draws the opponent in, around, and ultimately out.

Lesson: *An attacker swings at your temple. Slide swiftly in front of the blow, inside its circling trajectory, literally giving your opponent a hug—though an exceptionally well-timed one. Continue her rotation and redirect her momentum outward. Her balance upset, she spins and falls.*[48]

IF THE MARKET PULLS, BECOME ONE WITH THAT PULL — that's the essence of aikido politics' second pillar. The power of markets is hard to overstate; resisting is often futile. But directing markets' energy to sustainable ends holds great promise.

Amory Lovins and his colleagues put their fingers on this promise in their 1997 book *Factor Four:*

> Markets are very good—all too good—at what they do. The modern market economy harnesses such potent motives as greed and envy; in fact, as Lewis Mumford caustically noted, all the seven deadly sins except sloth. (Perhaps he was overlooking the entertainment industry.) But so effective is the profit motive that perhaps markets headed for unsustainability can best be redirected through creative use of market forces themselves, to harness their ingenuity, rapid feedback and diverse, dispersed, resourceful, highly motivated actors.[49]

Besides, directing markets is sound economics. Markets rarely operate in the real world as they do in textbooks. They are blind to nature, frequently dominated by monopolies, hamstrung by poor information, and distorted by incentives split among market actors. Governments, furthermore, sometimes prevent markets from operating at all. As a result, business as usual in the Pacific Northwest yields outcomes for society that often amount to "retail sanity and wholesale madness": Individuals respond rationally to the incentives and opportunities before them, but the collective result is bad for everyone.

Cunning use of market aikido—entering the center of the market's vortex and, through leverage well applied, sending it flying in a new direction—can correct market failures and create markets where there were none, effecting dramatic gains for sustainability. And across the Northwest and beyond, such innovations are emerging in encouraging ways.

6. CREATE MARKETS FOR CONSERVATION

Because they tap the expertise of millions of people, markets are brilliant at distributing commodities. Well-applied market aikido can harness this potential—instead of fighting against it—to find remedies for environmental ills.

The paragon of righting market failings with new markets is the US Environmental Protection Agency's sulfur dioxide program. Every year since 1995, the agency has issued pollution permits in declining numbers to regulated facilities. Each permit gives its owner the right to emit one ton of sulfur, and companies can trade permits like so many pork bellies. The program, which has helped halve emissions from these facilities, has stimulated a cheap cleanup: analysts forecast the value of each permit at $600 in 1992, but permits sold for $130 at the Chicago Board of Trade in late 2000. Northwesterners are forging similar markets to respond to challenges as diverse as reducing climate change and restoring dewatered rivers, overgrazed valleys, and depleted fisheries.[50]

The Oregon and Washington Water Trusts have begun prying open a market for water rights, braving the most convoluted, anticonservation thickets in all of Northwest resource law. Farmers do not own river water, only the right to use it, and they cannot sell water they save through improved efficiency. Worse, if they fail to use their full quota, they risk losing it. Predictably, many Northwest rivers run dry: in 80 percent of Oregon's watersheds, landowners' rights exceed what rivers can provide in late summer without sacrificing the minimum flows needed by fish and wildlife. The water trusts have found ways to pay landowners to leave water in streams, along 416 miles (669 kilometers) of Oregon rivers in 2000, for example. But only opening true water markets—by safeguarding minimum in-stream flows and allowing water users to trade rights above this threshold—would break the vicious circle of wasted water and dying rivers.[51]

Similarly, transferable grazing permits would turbocharge the emerging market for rangeland conservation. Holders of grazing permits for federal lands in the Northwest states also operate under a use-it-or-lose-it policy. For decades, conservationists have asked the federal government for grazing reforms on federal land, to no avail. Siding with ranchers, who view their long-held grazing permits as something close to property rights, conservationists could push instead to institute the principle that permits, though not true property rights, should nonetheless be tradable—and retirable—through transactions between willing buyers and willing sellers, at fair market value. Because the estimated value of all such permits in the region is only $252 million, public and private funds could readily free federal lands of livestock—if such an extreme change is ecologically warranted—without the controversy of mandatory range reform.[52]

Beginning in 1993, the Idaho Watershed Project began attending auctions of grazing permits for state lands. Intending to leave the land untouched by livestock, the project bid highest more than 30 times, but the state, accustomed to granting the permits to local ranchers after perfunctory bidding, refused to honor those bids. Finally, in January 2000, the state recognized the project's right to participate in the auctions. Since then, the project has bought grazing reprieves for 12,000 acres (4,900 hectares) of degraded rangeland, and the Bonneville Power Administration, eager to offset salmon killing by its Columbia River dams, has paid to remove livestock from another 48,000 acres (19,000 hectares).[53]

Four innovative efforts in the region are developing entering throws for climate protection, though they will not gain momentum until governments mandate such protection. The Pacific Forest Trust of Boonville, California, arranges deals between property owners willing to leave their land in old forests, which absorb carbon dioxide, and polluters willing to pay to mitigate their emissions. The nonprofit Oregon Climate Trust supports efforts ranging from energy efficiency to tree planting, using funds—$8 million since 1997—that it receives from new power plants forced to offset their greenhouse gas emissions to comply with state law. Since 1998, the Greenhouse Gas Emission Reduction Trading Pilot, based in Victoria, has kept approximately 23 million metric tons of greenhouse gases out of the atmosphere by brokering trades between companies willing to emit less and those willing to pay more. Individuals, meanwhile, can pay Victoria-based Climate Partners to offset their personal emissions, initially by underwriting a national carpool matching service.[54]

Tradable quotas for fish regulate access to both Canada's and Alaska's halibut fisheries. If applied throughout the Northwest, the approach would have great promise for trimming the region's overbuilt fishing fleet and the waste of resources, fish, and human lives resulting from frenzied fishing during short seasons, whatever the weather. Canada and Alaska began distributing tradable quotas for halibut in the early 1990s, and the ensuing long season and rational market have helped make North Pacific halibut the region's model sustainable fishery.[55]

Urban policymakers are using new markets to concentrate development in urban centers, allowing rural landowners to sell their development rights to urban developers who want to exceed zoning caps. Meanwhile, the partial deregulation of electricity markets, whatever its downside, has at least created new niches for renewable power: more than a dozen cities, companies, and utilities are now buying certified green power from the Bonneville Environmental Foundation in Portland, and many others are selling sustainable energy too. These instances remain exceptions to the rule, but they demonstrate the impact of the entering throw. They show how the Northwest can tame capitalism's environmental excesses with a well-executed embrace of its principles.[56]

7. DEREGULATE PARKING

Northwesterners end more than 90 percent of their auto trips in free parking spaces—actually, not free; somebody pays. In fact, the Northwest paid an estimated $14 billion in 2000 to store vehicles during their 23 hours a day of downtime—more than it spent on fuel. But only about 10 percent of the parking bill is pay-per-use at meters, lots, or garages. Drivers pay another 40 percent, through rent and mortgages, for off-street parking at home. The other 50 percent is paid by their employers, businesses they patronize, and other citizens.[57]

Pay parking is rare because antiquated provisions in zoning and tax codes, along with misguided street designs, bloat the parking supply and glut the market. Entering throws to redirect present zoning codes, which mandate oceans of parking, would let supply contract until a market emerges and turns the massive hidden cost of parking into a new chance for northwesterners to save money.

The 16 most populous Northwest counties and cities all require off-street parking; suburbs require even more parking than cities. Office buildings must provide up to four spaces per 1,000 square feet (93 square meters) of floor space, and retail developers in much of the region must devote more space to cars than to shoppers. Besides distorting the cost of driving, mandated parking lowers a community's density by 10 to 30 percent, leaving residents dependent on their cars.[58]

A few jurisdictions have recently begun shrinking parking requirements. Portland exempts downtown residential development from required off-street parking, and Olympia has no minimum requirements in its downtown core. Both cities have also set maximum amounts for off-street parking. A simpler throw would be full deregulation, allowing the market to decide how much parking space to provide. Many new developments would end up with less parking, lowering costs, especially for new rental housing. And metering or otherwise charging for curbside parking would ensure that drivers pay for using public rights-of-way, an approach Vancouver, BC, has effectively championed.[59]

Where communities are still being laid out, streets can be narrow, eliminating on-street parking. Olympia plans to build residential streets as skinny as 13 feet (4 meters) in one fast-growing neighborhood—one-third the conventional width and a Northwest and national record—while Missoula, Montana; Eugene, Oregon; and Kirkland, Washington, have pinched some streets down to 20 or 24 feet (6 or 7 meters).[60]

These techniques would also work for existing developments. With no parking requirements, the owners of buildings now surrounded by concrete would have new choices: they could expand, sell land to others, or turn parking into plazas. Cities could convert some current on-street parking into broader sidewalks, landscaping, and bicycle or transit lanes. It might take ten years to absorb excess parking space, but scarcity—and a market—would develop.

Finally, the Northwest could eliminate inequitable tax provisions that favor driving over other transportation. At present, taxes encourage employers to supply free parking by treating it as a nontaxable fringe benefit. Under BC and Canadian law, free parking is taxable income, but Revenue Canada makes only token enforcement efforts. In the United States, meanwhile, employers may give employees parking worth $175 a month as an untaxed fringe benefit—equivalent to pretax income that exceeds $2,500 a year. They may also pay for transit fares, but only up to $65 a month.[61]

"Cashing out" employer-paid parking would further dampen driving. A full-fledged cash-out policy requires that employers who give workers a free parking space also let them choose to receive instead the parking's dollar value in cash. Tests of this policy in Los Angeles show that as many as two in five commuters take the money and leave their wheels. California's tax law now requires large employers to offer cash-outs. Late-1990s revisions to the US tax code instituted a weak, partial cash-out policy: it allows—but does not require—employers to offer cash in place of parking, and it makes such cash fully taxable. In greater Seattle, the federal government is supporting efforts by local jurisdictions to encourage businesses to offer this cash-out.[62]

8. SELL CAR INSURANCE BY THE SLICE
Owning a car is expensive, but driving one is cheap. Car insurance, for example, is sold like an all-you-can-eat meal

plan: once you've made the purchase, you may as well gorge. Just as for parking, dividing this large fixed cost of car ownership into a pay-as-you-go charge gives drivers a new chance to save money. Few discrete changes would so dramatically reduce driving—and the congestion, collisions, and pollution that driving entails.

Drivers pay an average of 5–6¢ a mile for auto insurance—only slightly less than they pay for fuel. The more you drive, the more likely you are to collide with something. Yet, concerned that odometer tampering would invalidate their billing systems, insurers calculating insurance rates have paid minimal heed to how much driving each household does. Consequently, car insurance overcharges those who drive little and undercharges those who drive much—in British Columbia, by up to $200 a year.[63]

Electronic odometers and wireless communication technology now give insurers a chance to sell insurance by the mile. Progressive Insurance, the fourth largest US car insurer, is testing "smart" insurance in Texas. Car owners enrolled in the Autograph test-marketing program let Progressive install in their cars devices that record and periodically transmit how far they go and even where and when they drive—all factors that influence accident risk. As for any other insurance policy, the company also weighs considerations such as driving record. In late 2000, Progressive, pleased with the test marketing, was considering a national rollout.[64]

A low-tech alternative would be for insurers to simply offer drivers the option of reporting their own mileage, with periodic odometer checks at filling stations. Advocates in Washington have promoted this entering throw to the state's insurance commissioner, and the Insurance Corporation of

British Columbia, a regulated provincial monopoly, has commissioned research on the subject.[65]

Neither the high-tech nor the low-tech approach forces anyone into distance-based insurance, but the dynamic of the market is likely to expand the popularity of such plans. As low-risk, low-mileage drivers leave the traditional insurance pool, traditional profit margins would decline and prices would rise, pushing more low-mileage drivers into the distance-based alternatives. An expanding spiral would gradually make distance-based insurance common, or even the norm. And that change would be an enormous victory for sustainability: households that pay for their insurance by the mile are likely to reduce their driving by 10 percent. The opening would then exist for governments to convert some lump-sum vehicle taxes, such as registration fees, to per-mile charges, giving northwesterners another chance to save money by driving less.[66]

An analogous aikido move would sell auto use itself by the mile and the minute, rather than by the car. Car co-ops and car-sharing companies in Victoria, Vancouver, Seattle, and Portland promise many households a way to shed one vehicle without sacrificing mobility. The pay-as-you-go plan reduces driving among participants, typically by one-third to one-half.[67]

9. EXTEND THE BOTTLE BILL

A new twist on an old idea can multiply the reuse and recycling of materials. The old idea is the bottle bill, or deposit-refund system, long standard for bottles and cans in British Columbia, California, and Oregon—jurisdictions that are home to more than half of northwesterners.[68]

The new twist is the German philosophy of holding manufacturers responsible for their wares and packaging as long as
these items exist. This "extended producer responsibility," or
"take-back," approach to solid waste means, in effect, that if
you make a consumer good, you own it forever. The consumer
merely rents it for the services it provides, and when those
services are done—say, after the last sip of soda pop—the good
goes back to its maker, who must reuse or recycle it.[69]

Extended-responsibility legislation, enacted in 1991, increased the recycling of packaging in Germany sevenfold in
five years, reduced per capita consumption of packaging by
13 percent overall, and revived reusable containers. Three-
fourths of the country's fresh produce, for example, is now
shipped in durable crates. As important, end-of-life responsibility has transformed product design: manufacturers strive
to eliminate anything that's hard to handle when their goods
come back, such as toxic components and parts difficult to
recycle or reuse. More than two dozen countries now require
"take-backs" for packaging, and a dozen are planning take-
backs for computers and other electronics.[70]

British Columbia is the Northwest's deposit-refund
pioneer, having enacted North America's first bottle bill in
1970. Oregon followed with the first US bottle bill in 1971.
It's amazing how a nickel refund motivates people: Oregon
and British Columbia both collect 90 percent of beer cans
and bottles, and Oregon collects a similar share of soft-drink
containers. In contrast, Oregon recycles only 30–40 percent
of drink containers exempt from the bottle bill, and Seattle,
with no bottle bill but one of the best curbside collection
programs anywhere, recycles just 61 percent of drink cans
and glass bottles.[71]

Though Oregon's bottle bill has changed little in a quarter century, British Columbia has since 1992 turned its deposit-refund program into a true take-back program, adding motor oil, paint, household solvents, pesticides, pharmaceuticals, and most types of drink containers not previously covered. The return rate for this last category soared to 77 percent in the two years after its inclusion. In other extensions of producer responsibility, King County, Washington, is experimenting with computer take-backs, and Oregon's Department of Environmental Quality has recommended applying this entering throw to carpeting and to mercury-containing lights and thermostats. European countries, meanwhile, hold car and appliance manufacturers responsible for "cradle-to-cradle" product stewardship.[72]

Finally, companies need not wait for government mandates but can instead seek profits in reducing waste. Some corporations active in the Northwest have voluntarily taken responsibility for their goods' entire life cycle, a step in converting their business from a product-sales model to a service-contracts model. Xerox, for example, leases most of its copiers and, when the leases end, refurbishes the equipment for reuse. Herman-Miller, a furniture manufacturer, reclaims and reconditions its products for resale. Carpet maker Interface leases floor-covering services rather than selling rugs. The company retains ownership of its carpet, which it installs as tiles to allow periodic replacement of worn segments. At its factories, Interface separates the worn tiles into their parts and remakes them.[73]

CURB HANDOUTS
Pillar 3

"Open and turn," the third pillar of aikido, charts a path around a frontal assault and, sneaking up on the assailant sideways, turns his aggressive force back on himself. This pillar, like the others, embodies nonresistance. "If your opponent strikes you with fire," said founder Morihei, "counter with water, becoming completely fluid and free-flowing. Water, by its nature, never collides with or breaks against anything. On the contrary, it swallows up any attack harmlessly."

Lesson: *An attacker strikes at your head from over his own, his hand coming down like an ax. Spin to his side to avoid his blow, and, as you do so, catch his descending arm. By continuing his arm's natural rotation—first down toward the ground, then backward toward his rear and, finally, up until his arm reaches the end of its range of motion—flip him completely over. The redirected momentum of his attack thus neutralizes him.*[74]

ACH YEAR, NORTHWEST GOVERNMENTS REWARD
activities that degrade the environment with billions of
dollars in cash, tax breaks, and sweetheart deals, making a
frontal assault on northwesterners' land, air, and water. But
the region can open and turn these counterproductive subsidies with a few well-executed moves.[75]

Built up gradually over decades of political deal making,
the Northwest's myriad subsidies—between them, Washington and Oregon alone have enacted 700 special exceptions
in their state tax codes—dampen the economy, deplete natural wealth, and often penalize working families. Together,
these policies form a juggernaut against sustainable living,
but the Northwest can sidestep the onslaught, sneak up on it
sideways, and flip it head over heels.[76]

Take endangered Columbia River salmon: In the head-
waters, federally subsidized clearcut logging and public-lands
grazing clog spawning gravels with silt. Downstream, farms—
many growing federally subsidized cattle feed with irrigation
water chipped in free by the state and delivered from dams
built with federal dollars—drain and pollute waterways. On
the floodplains, locally subsidized real estate developments—
developers rarely pay the full cost of roads and sewer lines—
pave watersheds, underwritten with federally subsidized flood
insurance. Still farther downstream, government-funded
salmon hatcheries—built to mitigate dams and the loss of
upstream habitat—combine with federally subsidized dredg-
ing of river channels to further interfere with natural conditions. All these forces, including hatcheries, contribute to the
decline of wild salmon. And that decline has forced an end to
most salmon fishing, which, true to form, has occasioned
new subsidies—aid for displaced fishermen and multimillion-

dollar programs to restore fish populations. Some say the Northwest cannot afford to save its salmon; perhaps it cannot afford to keep killing them.[77]

10. PAY FOR ROADS WITH DRIVING-RELATED FEES

Drivers need roads, bridges, parking spaces, police, ambulances, and other services, but they pay only part of the associated costs through fuel taxes, vehicle registration and license fees, or parking charges. Taxpayers—regardless of how much they drive—pick up the rest of the tab. Most Northwest jurisdictions enshrine in law the principle that *all* revenue from fuel and other vehicle taxes be spent on roadwork, but road spending often exceeds the revenue from these taxes. An aikido reform would enshrine the parallel principle—that *only* fuel and vehicle taxes go to the automotive infrastructure.[78]

In 1998, the Northwest states spent on roads almost $1 billion from sources unrelated to driving, including property, sales, and income taxes. This figure excludes what the region's cities and counties spend each year on services for motor vehicles, such as traffic policing, car fire protection, and traffic planning. In greater Seattle alone, such services amount to perhaps $300 million a year; the regional total may exceed $1 billion. Adding insult to injury, the revenue code also plays favorites toward cars. In British Columbia and Washington, buyers can subtract the value of trade-ins from the price of a new car before sales tax is calculated. And these jurisdictions and Idaho exempt motor fuels from retail sales taxes; in Washington in 1997, these two giveaways were worth $334 million.[79]

Northwesterners can do aikido on the overuse of motor vehicles not by standing against them—they are, after all,

incredibly useful machines—but through a countermove that
rests on the user-pays principle. Requiring that motor vehicles pay for all roadwork, coupled with evenhanded tax
treatment of cars and fuel, would push driving rates down
and give other modes of travel a fair chance.

11. LET DEVELOPMENT PAY ITS WAY

Federal, state, provincial, and local policies in the Northwest
foster sprawl by subsidizing home ownership and new development. In particular, they encourage northwesterners to live
in big houses on big lots and to invest in second homes, which
are often built on fragile slopes and shorelines. But charging
developers for more of the basic services their buildings
require, and fine-tuning federal spending and tax rules, would
diffuse this force. Again, the key is to sidestep the momentum of northwesterners' desire to own nice homes and to
instead seize on fairness, thereby redirecting that momentum
toward more sustainable housing choices.[80]

In much of the Northwest, public infrastructure is fully
used, so added households demand added facilities and services—schools, roads, water pipes, sewer and drainage, police, fire, and ambulance. To help pay for these necessities,
many jurisdictions charge builders "impact fees" for each
house or apartment. Nowhere, however, do the charges fully
reimburse local treasuries for the expenses of development.[81]

In Oregon's cities, fees to the builder of a typical new
three-bedroom single-family home range from $2,000 to
$10,000. Yet the full cost of providing basic support for such
a home is $30,000 to $35,000. Local taxpayers end up saddled
with the difference. In Washington, typical impact fees are
$2,500 per house, though by one reckoning, the infrastruc-

ture to maintain the previous level of service after a new house is added would cost $83,000—almost $3 billion a year statewide. Two-thirds of the total goes to roads. In Washington's Thurston County, for example, the costs of keeping up with growth come to about $1,200 per year per taxpayer. Since almost no Northwest jurisdiction has been able to keep up, northwesterners pay for growth partly in tax dollars and partly in overcrowded roads, schools, and other facilities.[82]

Charging developers full fare would make growth pay for itself; adjusting impact fees by location would deflect sprawl back toward urban centers. The costs of support for new houses on the suburban periphery are often twice as high as the costs of upgrading in-town infrastructure, but the low price of remote land is a strong magnet for developers. Impact fees that increase with distance from established urban services would counter this attraction, putting the public costs of sprawl into developers' ledgers and the price tags of outlying homes.[83]

Reforming two federal programs would further discourage dispersed development. Curbing or phasing out the US National Flood Insurance Program would work wonders for ecologically sensitive wetlands; the program offers subsidies that actually encourage home construction in harm's way, on floodplains and near exposed coastlines. And even a gradual shift of priorities in the US Forest Service's efforts to contain forest fires—away from saving remote ranches and vacation homes—would brake the proliferation of such rural sprawl in the fire-prone woodlands of the inland Northwest. Perhaps one-third of the quarter billion dollars or more that federal, state, and local governments spent fighting Northwest wildfires in 2000 went into saving private development. In one case, federal agencies spent about $21 million controlling an Idaho fire to save private buildings with an assessed value of only $3 million. The private insurance market would deter much building in fire-prone areas if the federal government made clear it would protect human life but not second homes.[84]

Adjusting federal tax laws would also slow sprawl. US income tax law allows taxpayers to subtract mortgage interest, property taxes, and homeowners' capital gains (earnings from rising land values) from their income before calculating their tax bill. These deductions totaled $87 billion nationwide in the United States in 1997. Partly because the deductions are larger for bigger, more expensive houses, more than half the benefit went to households with annual incomes above $100,000; as a result, the US government gives more housing assistance to families with six-figure incomes than to the poor. State income taxes, most of which are tied to the federal tax, increase the amount and inequity of these handouts. Oregon lost $383 million to homeowner tax breaks in 1996.[85]

The United States could do better by emulating Canada's tax subsidy for home ownership. Canadians receive an income tax credit for property taxes paid, but they may not deduct their mortgage interest. The same share of Canadians owns their homes as Americans, but Canadians live in smaller residences. The United States could head in this direction, for starters by gradually lowering the $1 million cap on the amount of mortgage interest that's deductible.[86]

More ambitiously, the United States could replace its mortgage interest deduction with an income tax credit that's equal for all homeowners and set at the average value of the deductions, roughly $1,200. Typical homeowners and the public treasury would see no change in cash flow, but the incentives and distribution of benefits would invert themselves. At present, the more you spend on housing—the bigger your house, lot, loan, and property taxes—the bigger the tax break. With a home ownership tax credit, in contrast, all homeowners would receive the same $1,200 benefit, and no one would have a tax incentive to spend extra on housing.[87]

12. CHARGE FULL PRICE FOR THE PUBLIC'S NATURAL RESOURCES

All the Northwest's water, almost all its minerals, and 77 percent of its land belong to the public, yet irrigators, miners, and loggers have always paid bargain prices for these natural resources. Insisting on a fair return to public coffers would channel these industries' impacts in constructive ways.[88]

Though water itself is free to those with rights to use it in the Northwest states, irrigators—who use four times as much as all other northwesterners combined—do pay for its storage and delivery. They don't pay the full cost, however—typically ten cents on the dollar for water from the US Bureau of Reclamation's irrigation works along Northwest rivers such as the Klamath, Snake, and Yakima—leaving 90 percent of the tab to taxpayers. Farmers pay about a penny for 1,300 gallons (4,921 liters) to the Bureau's Minidoka Project, which covers one million acres (405,000 hectares) of Idaho's Snake River Plain. The lavishly subsidized farms in the Bureau's Columbia Basin Project in eastern Washington, meanwhile, get so much cheap water pumped to them that some farmers have built hydroelectric plants in their irrigation canals. Gradually easing farmers off these subsidies would prompt dramatic gains in water conservation and river restoration.[89]

Curbing handouts to mining would ensure that only highly profitable mines are developed. Such mines are better for the environment, too, because their rich ores require less disruption to extract. At present, gold, copper, and other hardrock miners pay no royalties anywhere on Northwest public land. British Columbia, which mines more than the rest of the region combined, collects royalties on oil and gas but not on minerals. Similarly, the US government charges 12.5 percent royalties on oil and gas, at least 12 percent on surface-mined coal, and 10–15 percent on geothermal steam but nothing for hardrock minerals from public land. Worse, US citizens and corporations have a legal right to mine on most public lands. For only $5 an acre paid to the federal treasury, miners can make public land private property—a handout that has, over time, deprived the United States of assets worth tens of billions of dollars.[90]

To capture the full value from public timber in places where logging is appropriate, managers can establish strong environmental standards, carefully calculate the government's cost for each sale, set that amount as the minimum bid, and request sealed bids for permission to log. The BC Ministry of Forests, the region's largest landowner, administratively sets rates for logging, often below market values. For 1997, most credible estimates of the resulting annual subsidy fall between Can$840 million and Can$2.6 billion. The US Forest Service, the region's second-largest landowner, auctions most of its timber but accepts bids far below its own costs, which include building roads. In 1997, some 26 of the 35 national forests in the US Northwest lost money on timber, generating $83 million of red ink all told. Halting these losses would more fully reflect the value of the public's forestlands.[91]

SLOW POPULATION GROWTH
Pillar 4

"Aikido," said founder Morihei, "*begins and ends with breath.*" "*Breath-power techniques*" form the art's fourth pillar. In aikido's spiritual teachings, breath is the universal force of life upon which students may draw to overcome the brute strength of any opponent. In less poetic terms, breath-power is exquisite timing and concentration of energy on the right leverage points.

Lesson: *The breath-power technique called "heaven and earth" begins like the playground game in which two children on a beam hold hands and try to throw their partner off-balance without falling themselves. Kneel facing your opponent as she grips your wrists from below. Yielding to that assault, lean back, drawing her off-balance. Then, to keep her off-balance, shift your own position several times—not with raw force but in swift, sudden bursts synchronized with your own breathing—to topple her.*[92]

I F THERE WERE BOX SCORES FOR POPULATION GROWTH, the Northwest's pace since 1990 (1.9 percent annually) would put the region in the middle of the Third World, leading India, neck and neck with Egypt, and gaining on Ecuador. Expanding ranks of inhabitants—15.5 million and counting—are responsible for most of the Northwest's increase in energy and water consumption, solid waste generation, and greenhouse gas emissions, along with about half the region's growth in traffic and suburban sprawl. How much northwesterners consume apiece matters as much or more, of course, but population remains a determinant of the Northwest's sustainability.[93]

Recent growth has come not purely from conscious choices to have children or to move northwestward, but also from flaws in public policy. Well-timed pressure on the right leverage points can slacken its pace. During the 1990s, 68 percent of Northwest growth came from people moving into the region, though over the span of decades, almost as much has come from natural increase (births minus deaths). Natural increase is simpler to tackle than migration, which always comes in fits and starts. Besides, births matter not only to the Northwest's future but to the globe's as well, whereas migration simply shifts population pressures. So natural increase is an appropriate leverage point.[94]

The Northwest can, and has begun to, slow natural increase, not by limiting people but by sustaining them. This approach is both ethical and effective. A close reading of the evidence reveals that rising numbers of humans are a symptom of deeper maladies, including neglect of children and women. Consequently, if the Northwest takes better care of people, natural increase will take care of itself. In particular, the region can concentrate its energies on three leverage points—reducing child poverty, preventing child sexual abuse, and expanding health insurance coverage for contraceptives— plus two opportunities for exquisite timing—making emergency contraceptives readily available during the three days after unprotected sex and making nonsurgical abortion available at the very beginning of pregnancy.[95]

13. TARGET CHILD POVERTY

Most northwesterners are already on the zero-growth bandwagon, planning families with two children or fewer. But birthrates among the disadvantaged raise the average: roughly one-third of natural increase in the Northwest would not occur if none of the region's families were poor. Women who live in poverty have 50 percent more children on average than more affluent women because, as women's education and economic situation improve, they opt for smaller families.[96]

Poverty singles out the young in particular for childbearing. Much of the region's discussion of teen births misses the fact that, statistically, teen births are a function of disadvantage: fully 83 percent of American teen mothers grow up in low-income families. Teenagers gave birth to one-tenth of the Northwest's newborns in 1998, accounting for 24 percent of natural increase that year. As economic disparity expanded in the Northwest between 1979 and the mid-1990s, the timing of childbearing became a class issue. Just as income prospects diverged, so did childbearing patterns. The haves in the new economy began waiting until after graduate school to have children; the have-nots began during high school.[97]

To alleviate population pressures in the Northwest, therefore, the most effective breath-power technique would guarantee young people a fair start. A remedy for child poverty would weave the Northwest a social safety net of a new variety. The region's welfare reforms of the mid-1990s cleared away ossified social service schemes but left little behind as a ladder of opportunity. Possible rungs for that ladder abound, rungs that emphasize personal responsibility. California now guarantees college tuition to low-income students who finish high school with a C average or better. And economists are designing programs to help poor families obtain assets, since most of the rise in inequality in the region stems from disparities in ownership rather than in earnings.[98]

Even subtle changes to public policy, such as expanding the earned income tax credit in the United States or indexing minimum wages to inflation, as Washington State has done, can slash the poverty rate. The US Social Security system has cut senior poverty by two-thirds since 1960—one of the greatest poverty reductions ever, anywhere—and the credit for much of that achievement goes to the mundane 1972 reform of indexing benefits to inflation. Typical seniors in America now get $17,700 a year in aid from the federal government; typical children get $2,500. Add state and local spending, and these figures still favor seniors three to one. Northwesterners don't begrudge people at the end of life a secure retirement; why should they begrudge people at the beginning a secure childhood?[99]

14. PREVENT SEXUAL ABUSE

If poverty is the principal cause of teen births, sexual abuse is its silent partner. Two-thirds of school-age mothers have survived childhood rape or molestation—three times as many as among all teenage girls. And one-fourth of school-age moms go on to have at least one additional child before their 23rd birthday.[100]

Abuse survivors often look on reproduction as a way to heal, a chance for redemption. The profile of a statistically average school-age mom shows why: Beginning just before her 10th birthday, she is repeatedly molested by her stepfather. At 13, she is raped by a 23-year-old acquaintance, the first of three rapes. She begins voluntary sex—if you can call it that—at 14. Her partner is 19; he promises her love and protection but sometimes beats her. She changes partners frequently and becomes pregnant before her 16th birthday with a different 19-year-old man.[101]

Abuse puts children at risk for further abuse. It corrodes their self-esteem, making them desperate for approval, affection, and safety, and teaches them to expect violation as the price of these birthrights. For a girl thus victimized, the thought of having a baby can seem like a chance for a fresh start. Alleviating poverty helps prevent abuse, because destitution creates the conditions in which much abuse occurs—insecurity, isolation, dysfunctional families, emotional disorders, and substance abuse. Poor children are many times more likely to be sexually abused than better-off children.[102]

A Northwest aikido tactic can also concentrate on fully funding child protection agencies, giving them clearer priorities, and unburdening them of the mountains of paperwork that keep workers at their desks rather than spending time with at-risk kids. A recent independent review in Washington reveals, as have most reviews elsewhere, a child protection agency in which staff are overloaded and have not been told whether keeping families together or safeguarding children should take precedence. These factors drive widespread employee burnout and rapid job turnover. Only half the reports of child abuse and neglect in Washington State are investigated, and experts believe that most abuse is never reported at all.[103]

As important, the region can monitor sexual abuse as rigorously as it monitors other crimes—or as its public health authorities track diseases. For these issues, the region compiles detailed information according to standard definitions and methods, generating a vast body of data that has helped reveal what works to fight crime and improve health. Without such monitoring, the region will never know how to invest in keeping kids safe. A first technique would emulate and improve on Washington State's Case Management Information System, which is among the best abuse-monitoring systems on the continent.[104]

Raising awareness would also help stem abuse. Six-year-olds have a better chance of knowing what to do if a stranger offers them candy than if a trusted adult tries to rape them. Sexual assault by a parent or parent substitute is 200 times more common than abduction by a stranger. The best prevention programs break the code of silence on which victimization thrives; they teach children a concrete body-safety rule to recognize abuse and then teach them to resist and report it.[105]

15. EXPAND INSURANCE COVERAGE FOR FAMILY PLANNING

The share of births from unintended pregnancies appears to have dipped during the 1990s after rising during the 1980s. Still, roughly 1 in 12 babies born in the Northwest are unwanted at conception, conceived accidentally by women who plan to have no children, or no more children. Another fifth or more of Northwest births result from pregnancies that the mothers regard as mistimed. These births, many of them to teens, usually happen one to three years earlier than desired.[106]

Experience in British Columbia shows that expanding insurance coverage for contraceptives is an effective breath-power technique for making unintended pregnancies less common. BC's universal health care system guarantees contraceptive coverage for all; at last count, unintended pregnancies were 40 percent rarer in Canada than in the United States. Since 1999, California and 13 other states have required all private insurers that pay for prescription drugs to cover the five prescription contraceptives: birth control pills, hormonal implants and injections, IUDs, and diaphragms.[107]

But millions of northwesterners still have medical insurance that pays for childbirth but not for contraception. In Washington, for example, even among the women who are enrolled in large, mainstream health plans, fewer than one in four are covered for all prescription contraceptives. (In contrast, nationwide, more than half of all prescriptions for the impotence drug Viagra are partly underwritten by health plans.) This penny-wise, pound-foolish approach to reproductive health puts highly effective methods such as hormonal implants out of reach for those who cannot afford the upfront cost. Health insurers would save money by covering prescription contraceptives, because accidental pregnancies are expensive. The cost to an insurer of a single delivery would pay for 15 years of contraceptives.[108]

In July 2000, a Seattle pharmacist brought a class-action lawsuit against her employer for sex discrimination, arguing that insurance plans covering most prescriptions must include contraceptives. In late 2000, the US Equal Employment

Opportunity Commission ruled in a similar suit that employers who cover preventive medicine must cover prescription contraceptives. In early 2001, Washington's outgoing insurance commissioner mandated coverage of contraceptives in that state, though the mandate was then put on hold for another year. But employers can get ahead of the courts by joining the hundreds of Northwest companies whose health plans cover all contraceptives. And Northwest state legislatures and the US Congress can pass the bills introduced in recent years to mandate equality in prescription coverage: during their reproductive years, American women now pay 68 percent more than men for prescription drugs.[109]

Because many northwesterners—13 percent among women of childbearing age in Washington, for example—lack insurance, the region could further bolster its private insurance market with publicly funded contraception programs. In the Northwest states, public support for family-planning services helps women prevent more than 50,000 unwanted pregnancies each year. Yet US federal support for family-planning services declined sharply during the 1980s and has yet to recover the lost ground. Some 55 percent of low-income Washington women who need contraceptive services lack access to a federally supported family-planning clinic.[110]

16. BROADEN ACCESS TO EMERGENCY CONTRACEPTION

Each day, more than half a million Northwest couples have sex; most of them do not aim to conceive a child. In the heat of passion, perhaps 40,000 of these couples dispense with birth control and take their chances on pregnancy; in some 2,000 more cases, a condom inadvertently tears or slips.

Almost 60 Northwest women become pregnant each day from condom failure alone. For such occasions, a Washington program has demonstrated a timely way to arm sexual partners with emergency contraception: the "morning-after" pill. Extending the program across the region would make unintended pregnancies much more rare.[111]

If taken within 72 hours of unprotected sex, emergency contraception—two special doses of hormones used in birth-control pills—prevents pregnancy. Though it has been available from doctors in the Northwest for 30 years, relatively few women have used it. For one thing, scheduling a special doctor's appointment within three days of a slipped condom is no easy feat, especially if a weekend intervenes. For another, many northwesterners have no idea that the option exists, or they decide to take their chances.[112]

Western Washington boasts a breath-power program that has tilted the balance in favor of emergency contraception more than perhaps any other initiative in the world. Launched in 1997 by a coalition anchored by the Seattle nonprofit PATH (Program for Appropriate Technology in Health) and since embraced by health-care and pharmacy institutions, this effort makes the morning-after pill available from any druggist who signs on to the voluntary program—with no appointments and no need to squeeze the errand into medical office hours.[113]

Under a Washington law that allows pharmacists to directly provide certain prescriptions through prior arrangements with individual medical practitioners, Washington's program has trained more than 800 pharmacists and, at last tally, was distributing roughly 750 prescriptions a month. At one chain pharmacy, prescriptions for emergency contraception increased 60-fold under the program. In its first year, the program targeted its advertising to women in the Puget Sound area, raising awareness of the technique as a backup to other methods. On very conservative assumptions, pharmacy distribution of morning-after pills in Washington is preventing 42 pregnancies each month, roughly half of which would have ended in abortion and half in births. Washington recorded one of its largest-ever declines in abortions in 1998, in part thanks to this program.[114]

PATH is now replicating the program in eastern Washington, and organizations in Alaska, Oregon, and California are following Washington's approach. British Columbia also inaugurated pharmacy access to emergency contraception throughout the province in late 2000. On a less optimistic note, retail giant Wal-Mart refuses to stock emergency contraceptives in its 90 Northwest pharmacies, fearing reprisals from the drug's most vocal opponents.[115]

A similar aikido move would expand women's access to very early abortion by granting government approval to the drug mifepristone (often referred to by its laboratory name RU-486). The United States completed this move in September 2000. In Canada, the BC government has pushed Ottawa to approve mifepristone for use there, and in mid-2000 a Vancouver, BC, gynecologist began conducting the necessary clinical trials.[116]

Developed in 1980 in France and used since then by more than half a million women in Europe and Asia, mifepristone ends pregnancies early by inducing something akin to a natural miscarriage. According to women who participated in the American clinical trials, it is more private, less invasive, and more natural-feeling than surgical abortion. Still, it is not "easy," as some critics have worried; mifepristone abortions typically involve painful cramping and heavy bleeding. What's key about medical abortion is its timing: it takes effect the instant a woman becomes pregnant. The availability of this choice encourages women and their partners to test for pregnancy very early: they can then choose whether to end the pregnancy or to start early prenatal care.[117]

GREEN THE TAX CODE
Pillar 5

Used to subdue an adversary, the "pinning techniques" of aikido's fifth pillar are familiar to anyone who's watched a police show in which an officer twists a villain's arm behind his back, wrist cocked. Improperly applied, pins can seriously injure the opponent; properly applied, they allow firm control of aggression and even limber up the attacker by stretching the muscles and joints. Pins are best executed gradually, with minimal force.

Lesson: *An assailant grabs for your right arm with his right hand. Intercept his hand as it passes with your own left hand, grasping the back of his hand. Your palm should be across his knuckles, your thumb on his palm between his thumb and fingers, and your fingertips wrapped around the knuckle of his little finger. The force of his thrust, redirected by your grip, causes his wrist to bend backward into a right angle and twist his arm the "wrong" way.*[118]

TAX CODES ARE THE AIKIDO PINS OF THE ECONOMY. As awesomely powerful as they are painful, they change almost every price in the marketplace, influencing the deci- sions of millions of consumers and businesses. When you tax something, you get less of it. So what does the Northwest tax? Mostly things northwesterners want more of: paychecks (payroll and income taxes), commerce (sales and business taxes), and investment (property tax). In contrast, many things northwesterners want less of remain untaxed: pollution, con- gestion, sprawl, and resource depletion. The tax system man- ages to send the wrong signals to almost everyone, yielding a Northwest that is both poorer and less livable.[119]

An approach taken to reform taxes in Europe, called tax shifting, uses taxes as aikido pins for sustainable economies. Nine European governments have begun reducing taxes on "goods," such as paychecks, and replacing the revenue, dol- lar for dollar, with taxes on "bads," such as toxic waste. And the move has helped both economy and environment.[120]

Environmental taxes put hidden costs—such as childhood asthma worsened by pollution—onto business ledgers and consumer receipts. They make prices tell the ecological truth. To quote the *Economist*, "Green taxes are good taxes." Some 2,500 economists, including eight Nobel laureates, have en- dorsed tax shifting as a response to global climate change, and the idea is gaining adherents in the Northwest. The Oregon legislature came close to passing a bill in 1999 to establish a task force on tax shifting; it is considering similar legislation for 2001. And in March 2000, British Columbia launched a pilot tax shift affecting the burning of sawmill waste.[121]

Tax shifting is a menu, not a prescription, and the menu is as long as the region's tax codes. A top-to-bottom overhaul of the Northwest's public finances could gradually replace most existing taxes with green alternatives, making long-term sustainability a regional priority. But opportunities also abound for narrow starter shifts in tune with the day's politics.

17. TAX POLLUTION, UNTAX ENTERPRISE

Each year, northwesterners send more than 3.5 billion pounds (1.6 billion kilograms) of harmful substances—100 million pounds (45 million kilograms) highly toxic—into the region's air, water, and land. This pollution causes hundreds of premature deaths yearly in the region and contributes to other ailments. The region's innumerable combustion devices also unlock from fossil fuels about 200 million tons of carbon dioxide each year; added to the atmosphere, this gas now hastens climate change.[122]

Taxing—even incompletely—the society-wide drip and hiss of pollution would allow governments to slash charges on profits and paychecks, charges that sap enterprise and work. And the infrastructure for pollution taxes is already sturdy enough to begin a decades-long transition in their direction. Most jurisdictions in the Northwest already require factories and other major polluters to report some of their emissions, and most charge these polluters administrative fees. Washington levies a small tax on oil and other hazardous substances and another on packaged foods associated with litter. California and Oregon now require pesticide users to report the chemicals they spread on the land, and a tiny tax on pesticides helps pay for California's reporting program.[123]

Where pollution comes from a factory, the region can build on top of existing regulatory fees to tax every pound of pollution and toxic waste emitted into the air, water, or ground. But pollution that does not come out of a smokestack or other fixed source is a growing menace. To tame the rising share of nonfactory pollution, the region can tax agrochemical sales and tailpipe emissions. At the regular air-quality inspections required in the region's metropolitan areas, officials can bill drivers in proportion to their emissions and miles driven. Such pollution-tax pins, set at rates that reflect the pollution's damaging impacts, would raise more than $3 billion a year regionwide. That sum would be enough to eliminate most business taxes: corporate income taxes in British Columbia, Idaho, and Oregon; BC's corporate capital tax; and Washington's business and occupations tax.[124]

Pollution taxes on this grand scale would double the price of many pesticides, boost prices of consumer goods such as nonrecycled paper, and make driving more expensive—by $135 a year per car, on average. A few heavy polluters would probably leave the region or shut down, but most firms would benefit. In fact, a pollution tax shift would strengthen the Northwest's stature as a magnet for nimble, low-pollution companies at the economy's vanguard. And the Northwest can apply pollution taxes slowly, perhaps starting with a tax on the most toxic substances, one that pays for a tax reduction divided between employers and employees. Or the region can begin with a slim tax on fossil fuels levied in proportion to their carbon content. Even a tax of $10 per ton of carbon dioxide would likely reverse the rise in climate-changing pollutants now under way in the region.[125]

18. TAX RESOURCE DEPLETION, UNTAX INCOME

To leave more money in northwesterners' paychecks and pocketbooks and to invigorate conservation and recycling

throughout the economy, governments could trim income and
sales taxes and make up the difference from levies on water,
hydropower, timber, and minerals. Industrial extraction of
these resources—the economy's feeding end—causes a disproportionate share of ecological degradation.

To reflect the cost of decimated salmon runs and other
consequences of damming rivers, for example, Northwest
jurisdictions could follow Idaho's lead by taxing hydropower.
Furthermore, governments could prepare for any deregulation of power markets that awaits the Northwest and—
through price-triggered taxes on private dams—gain from
windfall profits that deregulation could bring to the region's
dam operators. Just as oil and gas royalties pay for two-thirds
of Alaska's government, hydropower royalties could help pay
for other Northwest governments, lessening the need for revenues from existing taxes. Like BC's tax on windfall profits
from natural gas extraction, hydropower taxes could be mi-
nuscule when prices are low and rise as prices rise.[126]

Northwest governments could turn existing timber taxes
into true environmental levies. All Northwest jurisdictions,
except Oregon, already collect modest taxes on standing private timber as a substitute for property taxes. All the jurisdictions could separate a harvest tax from a property tax, as
Oregon does, making it clear that there is no tax on growing
trees, only on cutting them down. They could also extend
such a harvest tax, as does Washington, to public as well as
private timber. And they could offer a lower tax rate for the
harvest of certified sustainable timber. British Columbia does
impose a tax on logging, but Ottawa effectively assumes this
tax burden by counting every dollar a company puts toward
the logging tax against the company's federal tax bill. If

Canada ended that exemption, the province would have an environmental tax on logging.

Taxing diversions of water from rivers, and its extraction from underground aquifers, would drive water conservation and safeguard aquatic ecosystems. A tax of just 6¢ per 1,000 gallons (3,785 liters) would have generated more than $600 million in 1995, mostly from irrigators, who use 80 percent of Northwest water. In Idaho, which pumps more water per person than any country in the world, it would offset about half the state's sales tax. Yet such a tax would raise the cost of an order of French fries from Columbia Basin potatoes by, at most, one-twentieth of a cent.[127]

All together, at substantial but reasonable rates, these and other "pins" on resource depletion—applied gradually—could generate $5 billion in the Northwest each year, enough to replace one-third of the state and provincial personal income and sales taxes. British Columbia could generate enough from natural resource taxes to exempt every family below the median income from provincial income taxes. Washington could cut its state and local sales taxes by one-third—a bold stroke for social equity, because Washington's extreme reliance on the sales tax gives it the dubious distinction of having the most regressive tax system in North America.[128]

19. TAX SPRAWL, UNTAX BUILDINGS

Most Northwest jurisdictions combat sprawl with the regulatory tools of land-use planning; none applies taxes to the same task. Yet shifting the property tax partially or entirely off buildings and onto land values would turn it into a powerful incentive for investment in city and town centers and adjacent neighborhoods. And that investment is the best alternative to sprawl, because urban decay is the mirror image of suburban creep. In every Northwest city, there is ample room for development around town centers and in close-in neighborhoods, where land speculators commonly hold many vacant lots and rundown, low-rise buildings.

A property tax is actually two conflicting taxes rolled into one: it's a tax on the value of structures and a tax on the value of the land under those structures. Taxing built structures discourages building; taxing land values encourages it, especially in urban centers, where land values are typically hundreds of times higher than in rural areas.[129]

To encourage construction of affordable multifamily housing, for example, Portland and Seattle already provide temporary exemptions from paying tax on the value of qualifying new buildings. Oregon applies property taxes to the value of timberlands but not to the value of timber growing there. And every jurisdiction taxes the value of farmland but not the value of crops growing on it. The logic of these policies is impeccable and merits extending to all buildings, as it was in western Canada between 1903 and 1913 and as it is now in Australia, Taiwan, and Pennsylvania.[130]

Taxing sites but not buildings would turbocharge growth management, spurring development of the most valuable locations in developed areas. Parking lots, a common holding pattern for land speculators, would give way to buildings. Supplies of apartment and office space would increase. Rental prices would moderate. Lot-by-lot analysis in three counties, two in Washington and one in Oregon, suggests that a complete shift of the property tax off buildings would more than double taxes on parking lots and vacant lots, increase taxes by up to one-quarter on car-oriented commercial strip development, and moderately reduce taxes on pedestrian-oriented neighborhood shopping districts. It would reduce taxes by about one-third on the most land-efficient forms of housing, apartments and condominiums, and by about 5 percent for most single-family residences.[131]

A full-fledged aikido pin on land values would turn urban growth inward, and it would bring economic benefits by stimulating investment. And this reform is not all or nothing. States and provinces, for example, could simply give localities authority to reweight their property tax bases between land and buildings. Cities given that option could exert tremendous leverage on their own. They could end land speculation in their cores, and induce a burst of new development that would concentrate growth. Similarly, leaders could move only part of the tax burden off buildings or, if a property tax reduction is warranted, employ the same principle by lowering the levy on buildings but not on land. In British Columbia and Montana, which tax different classes of property differently, officials could restrict the reform to commercial zones.

20. TAX TRAFFIC CONGESTION, UNTAX COMMERCE

The next time you're stuck in traffic, think of Soviet bread lines. Socialist planners believed bread should be cheap, so they commanded the economy to make it. What little bread farmers and bakers made, the government sold for a pittance. Demand far exceeded supply, and, without any price mechanism to stimulate production or moderate demand, shoppers began paying with their time: they stood in line. Making more bread would not have ended Soviet bread lines; only creating a working market for bread could do that. The road transportation sector is among the world's largest remaining examples of Soviet-style central planning. Governments build the roads, then give away their use. Lacking any price mechanism, urban drivers pay for road use with their time, by waiting in traffic.

The best-kept secret among transportation experts is the near-universal agreement that variable tolls—known as congestion pricing—offer the only real solution to worsening gridlock. "Phantom tollbooth" scanners would deduct tolls from prepaid smart cards posted on cars' dashboards; the tolls would rise as rush hours approached and taper off as traffic dwindled. Demonstrated in Ontario and southern California, such tolls could generate more than $2 billion annually in the Northwest, offsetting many local taxes while easing the congestion that annually squanders more than 130 million hours of time and 143 million gallons (540 million liters) of gasoline in Northwest cities.[132]

The keys to public acceptance of this pinning technique are creating pilot projects for drivers to experience and first making toll lanes available where there are also free lanes. When new pay-per-use lanes opened on southern California's State Route 91, only 45 percent of drivers approved of congestion pricing; one year later, as many as 75 percent did. The idea of paying variable tolls was offensive; the reality was welcome. Just so, northwesterners would warm to toll roads after driving on them, and no sooner.[133]

Short of installing phantom tollbooths on existing roadways, traffic planners can accustom drivers to the technology by installing it at parking garages and ferry docks. (The Port of Portland is considering the technology for its new airport parking facility.) They can also introduce pay-to-drive as a way for single-occupant vehicles to travel in carpool lanes, many of which can accommodate more vehicles without slowing. Such high-occupant-toll (HOT) lanes have succeeded in San Diego and Houston.[134]

Congestion pricing is inching closer to reality in the Northwest. In Washington, tolls—which the state could easily make variable—will pay for a planned expansion of the Tacoma Narrows bridge. In Oregon, greater Portland's regional government recently began studying the potential for congestion pricing for each highway expansion project and is actively seeking a first chance to use variable tolls. And in late 2000, public pressure moved greater Vancouver's new transportation planning and financing authority, TransLink, to ask the provincial government for authority to use tolls to pay for transit and road projects.[135]

One reason to believe traffic taxes will ultimately arrive in the Northwest, even if piecemeal and incrementally, is the lack of alternatives. For example, even if the citizens of greater Seattle tax themselves almost $1 billion extra each year, for mass transit, roads, and other transportation improvements as specified in the region's approved master transportation plan, afternoon gridlock will still spread to almost half the freeway network in the central Puget Sound region by 2020. The time residents spend stuck in traffic will triple; average freeway traffic speed will fall to 21 miles (34 kilometers) per hour. Tolls, on the other hand, could tame congestion even while generating enough money to repeal local sales taxes.[136]

21. SPREAD CLEAN TECHNOLOGIES WITH "FEEBATES"

The Northwest's resource appetite is determined, to a surprising degree, by customers' choices when buying major new resource-consuming goods such as cars, appliances, and new buildings. Choosing a gas-guzzling new truck means filling that truck's tank for 15-odd years; building a drafty house bloats the region's energy budget for generations.[137]

Fuel-economy standards, appliance regulations, and building codes already set a baseline for new goods in the region, but a policy called feebates is better aikido. Still await-ing their Northwest debut, feebates are point-of-purchase incentives—fees charged to the buyers of less-efficient prod-ucts and rebates to the buyers of more-efficient ones—that systematically nudge consumers toward cleaner goods. As average efficiency increases, the feebates reset themselves around the new average, manufacturers raise their wares' efficiency to compete, and consumers set their sights still higher. Efficiency snowballs.

Just as other tax shifts leave government revenue un-changed, a feebate's fees pay for its rebates. And, like other tax shifts, feebates can be powerful pins: the cleaner the device, the bigger the rebate; the dirtier the device, the bigger the fee.

The closest the Northwest has come to feebates was in the early 1990s when the California legislature passed, but the governor vetoed, a new-car feebate, structured to favor cars that were safer for local air and global climate. Feebates then sat neglected in the region. Maryland tried a feebate on new cars briefly, before legal issues ensnared it. Since 1992, Ontario has charged a steep tax on gas guzzlers and given tiny rebates for gas sippers, but the program is not a true feebate. Similarly, energy and water utilities in the North-west have demonstrated the effectiveness of rebates for effi-ciency, but they've paid for these incentives from their own limited funds because they lack the authority to charge fees.[138]

Feebates counteract the market's blindness to environ-mental costs and three other documented market failures.

First, buyers—often choosing under pressure, as when the furnace goes out in midwinter—lack information about long-term costs. Second, a "payback" gap separates consumers from producers of electricity and other resources: appliance consumers typically demand a 2-year payback for investments in greater efficiency, while electricity producers build power plants expecting only a 20-year payback. Third, the motivation to minimize life-cycle costs is diluted by split incentives: landlords choose new water heaters, for example, but tenants pay the electric bills. These flaws cause massive, unnecessary investment in power plants, pipelines, and other facilities and amplify the ecological wake of daily life. Feebates untangle these twisted incentives, with surprising results. If the United States enacted feebates on new cars of only $70 per rated mile per gallon, new-car fuel economy would rise on average about 1 percent a year.[139]

Feebates could soon emerge from the shadows in the Northwest. Oregon endorsed national vehicle feebates to combat climate-altering pollution in 1995. And in 2000, British Columbia assembled a panel to advise the government on vehicle feebates and published a discussion paper on numerous feebate options. Unfortunately, protest from rural citizens at the mention of fees as high as Can$4,000 for new trucks has put the matter on hold.[140]

REVEAL WHAT'S HIDDEN
Pillar 6

"Rear techniques," the sixth pillar of aikido, heighten aware-ness of what is happening beyond the range of vision and prepare practitioners to diffuse an attack even when they're blindsided. A form of attentiveness to events we cannot see, they are associated in aikido teachings with presence of mind, good judgment, quick reflexes, and a "sixth sense" for antici-pating and averting trouble. Advised founder Morihei, "Rather than smashing your partner with brute force, dif-fuse an attack by leading it around you."

Lesson: *Stand with your arms at your sides. An attacker grabs your wrists from behind. Yield to her forward grab by bringing both hands forward while bending at the knees. In yielding, you use her own energy to pull her off-balance. As she falls toward you, slip to her side, under her arm, and let her tumble forward, head over heels, her lunge for your wrists turned into a graceful somersault.*[141]

NORTHWESTERNERS INHABIT AN ECONOMY THAT IS hardly local anymore: it roams the entire planet, burrows into its crust, and soars to the edges of the atmosphere and beyond. Consider the typical mouthful of food: it travels more than a thousand miles from farm field to dinner plate. In such an unbounded economy, the consequences of northwesterners' decisions—whether as workers operating factories, citizens electing leaders, or consumers choosing groceries—ricochet through vast institutions and make themselves felt in distant watersheds and communities, beyond our range of vision. Unintended consequences also make themselves felt locally, again often in ways we barely sense day to day. We scarcely notice the gradual waning of quality of life in our communities, for example, or the imperceptible ebb of the health and diversity of living nature.

The techniques of aikido politics' sixth pillar seek to expand the range of our senses, letting us see and better understand these elusive consequences, and letting us grasp the profound impacts of our actions on our neighbors and the millions of life-forms with which we share our place. These techniques create an artificial nervous system; they funnel new information into the marketplace and the political arena, exposing counterproductive practices in business and land management. Fully applied, mandatory pollution reporting, certification and labeling of sustainably produced goods, and monitoring of ecosystem health would help give the Northwest the sixth sense it needs to live within its planetary means.

22. BOLSTER THE RIGHT TO KNOW
In 1986, the US Congress inserted into its main law regulating toxic substances a provision requiring certain industries to

file annual inventories of toxic air emissions, water discharges, and waste disposal. These reports, catalogued by government agencies, allowed anyone to look up the pollution records of local manufacturing plants.

Feeling the heat of an informed populace, legislators, agency administrators, and plant managers replied with pollution prevention laws and voluntary reduction programs, which worked wonders. Between 1988 and 1998, reported releases of monitored chemicals fell 45 percent nationwide, and economic growth outpaced reported releases six to one in the Northwest states. When, in 1994, Canada required annual disclosure from major toxic polluters, British Columbia's reported releases declined 74 percent in just four years.[142]

Still, the accomplishments of these rear techniques are dwarfed by their potential. Expanding the laws' reach and closing loopholes would magnify the success of pollution reporting. Monitored chemicals remain a small fraction of toxics generated—perhaps even as low as 5 percent. The reporting laws in both the United States and Canada exempt all but large facilities, all but select industries, and all but 600—in Canada, 250—of the 70,000-odd synthetic chemicals circulating in the economy. Additionally, facilities report only what they themselves classify as waste, not all toxics used in production, so some companies reclassify chemicals to avoid reporting. Recognizing these weaknesses, both countries have gradually added chemicals and industries to their reporting lists to uncover previously hidden poisons.[143]

A model sixth-sense solution came in 1996, when Eugene, Oregon, adopted full materials accounting for toxic chemicals. The law requires facilities within city limits to submit a detailed accounting of hazardous chemicals from the moment they are purchased or produced to the end of their lifetime at the company. Every year, for each chemical, inputs must balance outputs. The law also mandates reporting for more than twice as many substances as the national statute—and for quantities as little as 500 times below national requirements.[144]

Public disclosure rules extend beyond toxics. Both the US Clean Air and Clean Water Acts include pollution reporting as part of their permitting processes. Any US citizen can examine a facility's permit history for its record of air emissions or wastewater discharges. British Columbia also makes such records public. Despite a rapidly growing economy, the Northwest states' emissions of the principal air pollutants have stayed flat for 15 years.[145]

Required reporting gives northwesterners the right to know who pollutes the region's water, but who uses it is another question. State laws require water users, including irrigators and municipalities, to measure the amount they divert from streams or pump from the ground. But no state enforces this provision. An early 2000 superior court ruling ordered the Washington Department of Ecology to begin enforcement, making the state the Northwest's test case for water-use monitoring. Requiring high-volume users to reveal the amounts they pump would accelerate conservation.[146]

The latest extension of the right to know has come in Oregon, where in 1999, lawmakers required all pesticide users to report each application. First enacted ten years ago in California, laws to report pesticide use give communities the right to know what chemicals are sprayed near schools, parks, and homes in their watersheds.[147]

23. LABEL WHAT'S SUSTAINABLE

On the cloud-covered central coast of British Columbia, old-growth forester Esmond Preus has been meeting with conservationists. But the meetings are not a protest. These conservationists have agreed to grant Preus's harvest—4,500 logging truckloads from government-owned land—the Forest Stewardship Council seal of approval. Preus will leave 40 percent of the forest standing, and the logs, processed and sold by certified businesses, will wear the council's label.[148]

With the Forest Stewardship label, Preus joins a growing number of Northwest aikido practitioners who are revealing the hidden consequences of their industries and turning buyer preference for environmental practices into profit. The technique is most effective when major buyers drive demand. Home Depot, the world's largest home improvement retailer, pledged in 1999 to sell only Stewardship Council–certified lumber by 2002. Added to the purchasing power of European buyers' groups, Kinko's, and others, Home Depot's pledge helped expand the market for certified wood sevenfold over the past two years.[149]

The potential is powerful, though it takes time for companies to shift practices. Many timber companies, like giant Weyerhaeuser, are opting for environmental standards created by industry groups or the International Standards Organization. These standards will not win products a place on Home Depot's shelves, however, because they do not trace timber from the forest to the customer's hands. Over time, Home Depot's pledge may lead companies like Weyerhaeuser to consider the Stewardship Council's more stringent label.[150]

Parallels to forest certification are emerging in other industries. The Marine Stewardship Council is a saltwater equivalent of the Forest Stewardship Council, writing rules for sustainable fisheries. The Unilever Corporation has committed to purchase only certified seafood by 2005—no small promise for the company that controls one-fifth of the market for boxed frozen fish in Europe and the United States. In fall 2000, Alaska's closely monitored salmon fishery became the first US fishery to gain the Marine Stewardship Council's seal, and its fishers hope the label will buy them access to certification-friendly markets, including the giant Unilever.[151]

Seattle and Portland both recently approved policies mandating that new or newly remodeled city properties follow the US Green Building Council's LEED (leadership in energy and environmental design) standard for nonresidential buildings. As initial projects demonstrate the economic viability of "green building," the industry is incorporating new ideas, such as recycled building materials, rainwater collection systems, and efficiency-maximizing designs.[152]

Renewable energy producers are using certification to stimulate creation of new power sources. In deregulated electricity markets, consumers can purchase certified "Green-e" renewable energy directly from suppliers. And a dozen Northwest utilities in regulated markets offer customers an option to pay a premium for certified energy. Contracts for renewable energy can translate into new wind turbines or solar generators in place of an oil, gas, or hydroelectric power plant.[153]

The veteran green label belongs to certified organic food. A decade of annual sales growth higher than 20 percent is convincing greater numbers of Northwest farmers to go organic. The US Food and Drug Administration's adoption of a national organic standard in December 2000 could further increase organic farming by making certification easier for

farmers and consumers to understand. The success of certified organic food underscores the potential of consumers' sixth
sense to overturn practices whose impacts ripple throughout
the economy.[154]

24. MONITOR LIVING SYSTEMS

Quietly, mostly beyond our range of vision, ecosystem integrity is unraveling. Rear techniques to repair the tatter would
evaluate the health of living systems and spur appropriate
action. One such technique, biological monitoring, can do
both. It uses living indicators, such as insects, fish, or plants,
to uncover the biological consequences of human decisions.
Already used to manage rivers worldwide, biomonitoring—
systematically applied and made the report card for resource
management in the Northwest—would drive dramatic improvements in the health of regional ecosystems.[155]

Ohio—whose fish populations were so depleted by 1880
that wardens believed "the total extinction of fish life is drawing near"—has used biomonitoring since the 1980s to diag-
nose river ills and speed recovery. The state relies on biological
indexes modeled after economic indexes like the Dow Jones
industrial average, but these indexes follow river organisms,
not companies. Such indexes told Ohio that, of stream and
river reaches meeting chemical water quality standards, nearly
half were unhealthy biologically; the indexes also helped pin-
point why. On the Scioto River, which runs through Columbus, for example, biomonitoring revealed that effluent from
wastewater plants was killing life downstream. In response,
plant managers instituted changes that raised downstream
health from "poor" to "good" and even "exceptional" over
a decade. Ohio has since made biological indexes the center-

piece of its clean-water strategy. The effects are manifest state-wide—in rising numbers of river miles now meeting Clean Water Act standards, greater abundance of native species, and recovering populations of endangered fish.[156]

Faced with their worst river crisis ever, the Northwest's water managers can follow Ohio's lead. Salmon populations have plummeted. Some 54 percent of Washington's—and 70 percent of Oregon's—rivers and streams are impaired according to chemical and physical measures. But if, as in Ohio, full biological assessments double such tallies, the Northwest's waters are actually in worse shape. Systematic biomonitoring, which is slowly catching on, would direct authorities' attention toward root causes and cures.[157]

Every Northwest state and British Columbia uses biological assessments to describe the health of some rivers, and Montana does so for wetlands; the information often drives specific land-use decisions. But no Northwest jurisdiction has yet set numeric biological targets for river health—beyond counts of bacteria that sicken people—or held authorities accountable for reaching the targets. Ironically, Idaho—under court order in the mid-1990s for failing to meet Clean Water Act provisions—now leads the Northwest in monitoring river health; it has applied biological indexes to almost 1,900 stream sites. Oregon has biological indexes for the Willamette River and Coast Range streams and is developing numeric biological criteria for Clean Water Act compliance. In addition to sponsoring watershed biomonitoring projects to evaluate forestry practices, British Columbia has made "ecosystem integrity" a top goal of its freshwater strategy.[158]

Biological monitoring is gradually spreading, among citizens and among agencies, and from waterways to land. University of Washington scientists have trained volunteers to monitor dozens of Puget Sound streams and are developing biological indexes for terrestrial ecosystems, starting with the inland Northwest's sagebrush-steppe. Schoolchildren in Washington are using similar techniques to examine neighborhood streams. And, research shows, volunteers' data are as reliable as professional scientists'. When authorities make the results of expanding biomonitoring efforts the mark of their own success, ecosystem health will begin the prolonged recovery so needed in the region.[159]

A PLACE TO STAND

Every aikido technique presupposes multiple attackers; the movements remain essentially the same regardless of the number of opponents. But the six pillars gain their full potential not in separate use but in their combination. The various throws, pins, rear techniques, and breath-power techniques together, as executed by masters, are almost unbelievable. They look like magic. Even diminutive aikido masters can handle four or more strong opponents at once.

Yet this mastery does not come from simply knowing the techniques; it comes from developing a stance, physically and mentally, that is profoundly relaxed yet charged with energy. The proper stance is supremely attentive to everything that is happening. From it flows readiness to seize fleeting opportunities and diffuse attacks, even attacks by several assailants. Deceptively simple, developing such a stance is one of the hardest parts of aikido.[160]

A IKIDO POLITICS IS ABOUT LEVERAGE. IT'S ABOUT small changes that make a huge difference, about acting on the hidden points in the Northwest's body of rules, institutions, and practices to shift the momentum of that body toward sustainable ends. Surprisingly disparate things turn out to be pressure points: handheld computers that arrange carpools, new prescribing privileges for pharmacists, expanded markets for water permits. With so many unexpected leverage points, aikido politics seems to thrive on paradox: dense, "unnatural" urban centers are a key to protecting both wildlands and global climate; alleviating child poverty slows population growth; monitoring living systems sets in motion political forces that help restore them. And, as a final paradox, aikido politics finds global leverage in local changes; by succeeding, the Northwest can inspire success elsewhere.

This Place on Earth 2001 describes two dozen techniques, but it's still a preliminary guide to aikido politics for a sustainable Northwest. In future editions, NEW expects to document other techniques and rank them with the help of dozens of knowledgeable northwesterners. This year's volume describes few techniques for reforming the region's antiquated water laws, for example. Or for restructuring the perverse and convoluted public financing systems for roads and transit spending. Or for speeding the region's shift to low-impact practices in agriculture, fishing, and forestry. It ignores entire categories of throws: voluntary changes in business accounting methods that set sustainability as a corporate objective; proven public education campaigns that curb waste; and changes not in specific policies but in the process of governance itself.

For example, perhaps other metropolitan areas need to emulate greater Portland's regional governing council if they are to achieve meaningful integrated planning. Similarly, the region's countless localities and overlapping agencies may need to cede power over some issues to higher, regional authorities to succeed at restoring Columbia River salmon. And swift progress toward sustainability may require improvements in democracy—reforms in how political campaigns are conducted or in the citizens' initiative process, which has recently outflanked legislatures in Oregon and Washington.

Our book does not address the role of leadership in aikido politics: the power that comes from defining public issues by setting stark challenges. In May 2000, for example, Oregon Governor John Kitzhaber issued an executive order declaring sustainability one of the state's highest goals. The order reads, in part, "The state of Oregon shall develop and promote policies and programs that will assist Oregon to meet a goal of sustainability within one generation—by 2025." This directive may not prove to have much leverage. It is neither a law nor an amendment to the state constitution; it simply directs state agencies to develop plans for improving their own internal environmental performance. Nonetheless, it does finally invoke sustainability as a top priority and declare an audacious timeline—"within one generation." If the public accepts this principle, it could set a popular standard against which to judge government actions.[161]

Neither does this volume indicate which techniques of aikido politics are most powerful. Increasing urban density, reducing child poverty, and overhauling the tax system tentatively stand out as the most promising. Unfortunately, they may also be among the most difficult to execute because they demand so much political finesse. Selling car insurance by the mile, bolstering the right to know, and rigorously monitoring ecosystem health may be easier first techniques for the region to master.

And finally, *This Place on Earth 2001* does not explore how best to combine aikido moves. The full potential of the listed reforms would be realized only if skillfully combined. Consider greenhouse gas emissions, which the region needs to cut by 80 to 90 percent within a century to lead the world toward climate stability. Climate-altering pollution would be reduced by:

- Communities that were increasingly compact, walkable, and tied together with cost-effective alternatives to driving alone.
- The reduced driving that results from selling insurance by the mile.
- A slowing of population growth brought on by safe, secure childhoods for all and universal access to prescription and emergency contraceptives.
- Protection and restoration of ecosystems, such as old forests, that soak up carbon dioxide.
- Thriving consumer markets in conservation, pollution reduction, and certified sustainable products, including renewable electricity.
- The energy conservation yielded by bottle bills and other forms of extended producer responsibility.
- The tremendous reductions in fossil fuel combustion, forest clearing, and other greenhouse gas generation that would result from elimination of taxpayer subsidies to driving, sprawl, and other high-impact activities.
- The even larger reductions in emissions that would come from comprehensive feebates and from shifting the bur-

den of taxation off paychecks and enterprise and onto pollution, resource depletion, and habitat disruption.

Mixed and given time to work, these catalysts might well bring the required decline in emissions. Indeed, their cumulative effect over decades might be a phasing out of fossil fuel use altogether in favor of renewable alternatives. Other aikido techniques used together can likely safeguard the functioning and diversity of the region's ecosystems, improve quality of life for time-crunched families, and expand economic opportunities for working northwesterners. Yet *how* to combine the moves is a question for another year's edition of this annual book.

What we hope this edition does is demonstrate the power, the opportunity, even the necessity of using leverage to throw the Northwest toward a way of life that can last. It may also show that doing so will have ripple effects far beyond the borders of this region of salmon, rivers, and rainforests. When the Greek mathematician Archimedes first defined the principle of leverage 23 centuries ago, he said, "Give me a place to stand, and I will move the Earth." He was not simply bragging. In a universe without fixed objects, an immovable point would confer enormous powers on someone with a long lever and knowledge of how to use it.[162]

Aikido politics is about leveraging Earthly movement, not in Archimedes's literal sense, but in the sense of turning the current of human affairs into a channel that leads to recovery for the nonhuman realm and continued flourishing for human communities. Northwesterners have a place to stand. If they master the leverage of aikido politics, perhaps they will move the world.

Acknowledgments

This Place on Earth 2001 owes its existence to the eleven books created by Northwest Environment Watch (NEW) since 1993 and to their contributors. NEW's research team, which pulled together this "best of NEW" collection, updated it, and added to it, consists of executive director Alan Thein Durning; editorial director Ellen W. Chu; research associates Joanna Lemly, Jennifer Tice (summer 2000), and Chad Westmacott; and research interns Angela Jones, Lynne Jordan, Ryan Phillips, and Shari Stieber. The findings here depend heavily on former research director John C. Ryan and some 40 past research interns. NEW could not have done its last seven years' work without them.

NEW thanks Adam Eisenberg of Emerald City Aikido, Seattle, for the chance to observe aikido in action.

For their helpful comments on drafts of this book, NEW thanks reviewers Jeff Allen, Lori Bielinski, John Charles,

Ralph Cipriani, Judith Chrystal, Bob Doppelt, Eben Fodor, Pat Franklin, Christine Hagerbaumer, Michael Harcourt, Jane Hutchings, Carole Joffe, James R. Karr, Todd Litman, Mike A. Males, Langdon Marsh, Dick Nelson, Mary O'Brien, Suzanne Poppema, Thomas Michael Power, Gordon Price, Roberta Riley, Karin Sable, Donald Shoup, David Stitzhal, Amy Taylor, Elisa Wells, and Sandy K. Wurtele. For all their hard work, we also thank our volunteers Elizabeth Atcheson, Peggy Austin, Jeffrey Belt, Ellen Caldwell, Roma Call, Peter Carlin, Mark Cliggett, John and Jane Emrick, Dean Ericksen, Tony Henderson, Ben Keim, Bill Kint, David Kowalsky, Norman Kunkel, Lyn McCollum, Steve Mack, Michael Montague, Laura Retzler, John Russell, Kathy Fong Stephens, Todd Van Horne, Leonard Wainstein, and Suzy Whitehead.

NEW is grateful to its board of directors: John Atcheson, Aaron Contorer, Alan Durning, Jeff Hallberg, Sandra Hernshaw, Cheeying Ho, and board chair David Yaden. NEW also thanks the board of NEW BC, our Canadian affiliate in Victoria: Sandi Chamberlain, Alan Durning, chair Cheeying Ho, Rick Kool, Heather McAndrews, and Donna Morton. We also thank the NEW BC staff: Donna Morton, executive director; Meredith Elliott, office manager; Michelle Hoar, communications and outreach coordinator; Zane Parker, project director; and Amanda Pawlowski, financial officer.

Financial support for Northwest Environment Watch comes from more than 1,000 members and donors and from the Brainerd and Bullitt Foundations; Mary A. Crocker Trust; C. S. Fund; Nathan Cummings, Hanlon, William and Flora Hewlett, Horizons, W. Alton Jones, Henry P. Kendall, Kongsgaard-Goldman, and Lazar Foundations, Merck Family Fund; David and Lucile Packard, Russell

Family, True North, Turner, Weeden, Winky, and the Hans and Elizabeth Wolf Foundations.

Besides the research team, NEW's staff while this book was in progress included Parke Burgess, development director; Rhea Connors, operations director; Tyesha Kobel, program coordinator; André Mershon, former program coordinator; Elisa Murray, communications director; Stacey Panek, membership coordinator; and Deirdre Stevenson, bookkeeper.

Not everyone at NEW subscribes to every idea in this book, but we all bear responsibility for any errors that remain. Except for typos and sentence fragments. Those are the editorial director's fault.

N O T E S

1. Population from US Census Bureau, "1990 to 1999 State Population Estimates: Annual Time Series," *www.census.gov*, Jan. 24, 2001; Statistics Canada (StatCan), "Population by Year," *www.statcan.ca*, Jan. 24, 2001. Gross state and provincial product estimated from US Bureau of Economic Analysis (BEA), "Regional Accounts Data," *www.bea.doc.gov*, Feb. 5, 2001; and BC Stats, "BC GDP at Market Prices and Final Domestic Demand, 1981–1999," *www.bcstats.gov.bc.ca*, Feb. 5, 2001. Canadian exchange rates and price deflators from *Canada Year Book 1999* (Ottawa: StatCan, 1998).

2. Alan Thein Durning, *This Place on Earth: Home and the Practice of Permanence* (Seattle: Sasquatch Books, 1996).

3. John C. Ryan, *State of the Northwest*, revised ed. (Seattle: NEW, 2000).

4. Jujitsu from US Ju-Jitsu Federation, "What Is Ju-Jitsu?" *www.usjujitsu.net*, Nov. 22, 2000. Aikido from John Stevens, *The Shambhala Guide to Aikido* (Boston: Shambhala, 1996).

5. Wind-power plant from Patrick Mazza, "The Advantages of Wind Power," *Seattle Post-Intelligencer*, Jan. 26, 2001.

6. NEW estimates in this chapter based on sources in notes 6–23, adjusted for population in 2000. Gross state and provincial prod-

uct increase estimated on the basis of BEA, op. cit. note 1; BC Stats, op. cit. note 1; and *Canada Year Book 1999*, op. cit. note 1. Gross domestic product of nations from *World Resources 2000–2001* (Washington, DC: World Resources Institute [WRI], 2000).

7. Population increase from US Census Bureau, op. cit. note 1; and StatCan, op. cit. note 1. Oregon Trail travelers estimated from Dorothy O. Johansen and Charles M. Gates, *Empire of the Columbia* (New York: Harper, 1957). Population of nations from *World Resources 2000–2001*, op. cit. note 6.

8. Growth of households estimated on the basis of average annual increment during 1990s from US Census Bureau, "ST-96-24R Estimates of Housing Units, Households, Households by Age of Householder, and Persons per Household of States: Annual Time Series, July 1, 1991, to July 1, 1996," *www.census.gov*, Dec. 1, 1999. New houses and apartments estimated on the basis of *Statistical Abstract of the United States 2000* (Washington, DC: US Census Bureau, 2000).

9. Growth of vehicle fleet—excluding motorcycles and trailers—and trucks' share of fleet estimated using late 1990s growth rates from US Federal Highway Administration (FHWA), "Highway Statistics Series," *www.fhwa.dot.gov/ohim/ohimstat.htm*, Jan. 18, 2000; Canadian Socio-Economic Information Management System (CANSIM) Time Series Database, "Road Motor Vehicle Registrations, Total, BC-D462188," and "Motorcycle Registrations, BC-D462191," *www.statcan.ca/english/cansim*, Feb. 7, 2000; and "Auto Tracker Statistical Report," Polk Company, Southfield, Mich., various editions.

10. Daily resource use from John C. Ryan and Alan Thein Durning, *Stuff: The Secret Lives of Everyday Things* (Seattle: NEW, 1997). Daily water use per capita ("consumptive use") and Idaho withdrawals per capita estimated from Wayne B. Solley et al., *Estimated Use of Water in the United States in 1995*, (Washington, DC: US Government Printing Office, 1998), at *water.usgs.gov/watuse/pdf1995/html/*; BC's water consumption estimated as comparable to Oregon's. Nation's withdrawals from *World Resources 2000–2001*, op. cit. note 6. Climate-changing emissions from John C. Ryan, *Over Our Heads* (Seattle: NEW, 1997).

11. Increase in developed land area in Idaho, Oregon, and Washington estimated from *National Resources Inventory Summary Report 1997*, revised ed. (Washington, DC: US Natural Resources

Conservation Service, Dec. 2000), at *www.nhq.nrcs.usda.gov/ NRI;* no comprehensive data on developed land area in British Columbia available for the 1990s.

12. Annual logging area in BC, where virtually all Northwest old-growth logging takes place, from Neville Judd, "Stumpage System Betrays BC Forests' True Worth," *Environment News Service,* Jan. 30, 2001.

13. Water use from Solley et al., op. cit. note 10.

14. Orcas from Robert McClure, "Risk of Orca Extinction Underscored in Analysis," *Seattle Post-Intelligencer,* Feb. 23, 2001.

15. Officially listed species from US Fish and Wildlife Service, "Species Information: Threatened and Endangered Animals and Plants," *endangered.fws.gov/wildlife.html,* Feb. 27, 2001; Committee on the Status of Endangered Wildlife in Canada, "Database of Listed Species," *www.cosewic.gc.ca,* Feb. 27, 2001; Washington Dept. of Fish and Wildlife, "Species of Concern in Washington State," *www.wa.gov/wdfw/wlm/diversty/soc/soc.htm,* Feb. 27, 2001; Oregon Dept. of Fish and Wildlife, "Oregon List of Threatened and Endangered Fish and Wildlife Species," *www.dfw.state.or.us/ODFWhtml/Wildlife/t%26e.html,* Feb. 27, 2001; and Idaho Dept. of Fish and Game, "The Idaho Conservation Data Center," *www2.state.id.us/fishgame/cdchome.htm,* Feb. 27, 2001. Unlisted species also faring poorly from BC Ministry of Environment, Lands and Parks (BC MELP), "BC Conservation Data Centre," *www.elp.gov.bc.ca/wld/cdc,* Jan. 1999 (now at *www.env.gov.bc.ca/rib/wis/cdc/*); Marta Donovan, BC Conservation Data Centre, Victoria, private communication, Jan. 19, 1999; Washington Dept. of Natural Resources, "Washington Natural Heritage Program," *www.wa.gov/dnr/htdocs/fr/nhp,* Jan. 1999; Jack McMillen, Washington Natural Heritage Program, Olympia, private communication, Jan. 14, 1999; The Nature Conservancy and Oregon Division of State Lands, "Oregon Natural Heritage Program," *www.heritage.tnc.org/nhp/us/or,* Feb. 1999 (now at *ocelot.abi.org/nhp/us/or/*); and Idaho Dept. of Fish and Game, "The Idaho Conservation Data Center," *www2.state.id.us/ fishgame/cdchome.htm,* Feb. 1999.

16. Total pollutants estimated on the basis of sources including US Environmental Protection Agency (US EPA), "Toxic Release Inventory Explorer," *www.epa.gov/triexplorer,* Oct. 21, 2000; *National Pollutant Release Inventory 1994–1998 Databases and*

Reports on CD-ROM (Ottawa: Environment Canada, 2000); US EPA, "National Air Pollution Emission Trends Update, 1970–1997," *www.epa.gov/ttn/chief,* Jan. 21, 2000; *Emissions Trends Viewer, 1985–1995,* CD-ROM 1.0 (Washington, DC: US EPA, 1996); Vesna Kontic, *Inventory of Authorized Discharges under the Waste Management Permit Fees Regulation 1994/95–1995/96* (Victoria: BC MELP, 1996).

17. CO_2 emissions estimated from US EPA, "EPA State CO_2 Inventories by Energy Source," *yosemite.epa.gov/globalwarming/ghg.nsf,* Feb. 28, 2001; and F. Neitzert et al., *Canada's Greenhouse Gas Inventory: 1997 Emissions and Removals with Trends* (Ottawa: Environment Canada, 1999), at *www.ec.gc.ca/pdb/ghg.*

18. Uniqueness of life on Earth from Peter D. Ward and Donald Brownlee, *Rare Earth: Why Complex Life Is Uncommon in the Universe* (New York: Copernicus, 2000); and Donald Brownlee, Dept. of Astronomy, University of Washington, Seattle, private communication, Oct. 20, 2000. Human protoplasm from Edward O. Wilson, "Is Humanity Suicidal?" *New York Times Magazine,* May 30, 1993. Increase in body size and lifespan from Robert William Fogel, *The Fourth Great Awakening and the Future of Egalitarianism* (Chicago: Univ. of Chicago Press, 2000). Population increase from US Census Bureau, "Historical Estimates of World Population," *www.census.gov,* Dec. 4, 2000. Increase of resource use from J. R. McNeill, *Something New under the Sun* (New York: Norton, 2000). Human influence on global climate from Intergovernmental Panel on Climate Change, *Climate Change 1995: The Science of Climate Change* (Cambridge, UK: Cambridge Univ. Press, 1996). Rate of extinction from Edward O. Wilson, *The Diversity of Life* (Cambridge, Mass.: Belknap Press, 1992). Synthesized chemicals within human body from Theo Colborn et al., *Our Stolen Future* (New York: Dutton, 1996).

19. The Northwest's role in reducing greenhouse gas emissions from Ryan, op. cit. note 10.

20. Conversion from horse to automobile from Carlos A. Schwantes, *The Pacific Northwest: An Interpretive History* (Lincoln: Univ. of Nebraska Press, 1989).

21. Emissions reduction based on energy consumption data from *State Energy Data Report 1994* (Washington, DC: US Energy Information Administration [EIA], 1997), at *www.eia.doe.gov; Detailed Energy Supply and Demand in Canada* (Ottawa: StatCan, 1960–1977); and *Quarterly Report on Energy Supply-Demand in*

Canada (Ottawa: StatCan, 1976–1995); and on carbon coefficients from A. P. Jaques, *Canada's Greenhouse Gas Emissions: Estimates for 1990* (Ottawa: Environment Canada, 1992); and *Emissions of Greenhouse Gases in the United States, 1987–1992* (Washington, DC: EIA, 1994). Population growth during 1950–99 from John L. Androit, ed., *Population Abstract of the United States* (McLean, Va.,: Androit Associates, 1983); "Estimates of the Resident Population of States: July 1, 1991 to 1993 and July 1, 1992 to 1993, Components of Change," press release CB93, US Census Bureau, Washington, DC, 1993; *Historical Statistics of Canada* (Ottawa: StatCan, 1983); *Population 1921–1971: Revised Annual Estimates of Population, by Sex and Age Group, Canada and the Provinces* (Ottawa: StatCan, 1973); *Intercensal Annual Estimates of Population by Sex and Age for Canada and the Provinces: 1976–1981* (Ottawa: StatCan, 1983); *Annual Demographic Statistics,* cat. no. 91-213 (Ottawa: StatCan, 1994); and US Census Bureau, op. cit. note 1; and StatCan, op. cit. note 1.

22. Vehicle trips estimated on the basis of *Highway Statistics 1999* (Washington, DC: FHWA, 2000), at *www.fhwa.dot.gov/ohim;* and *Transportation Energy Data Book,* 20th ed. (Oak Ridge, Tenn.: Oak Ridge National Laboratory, 2000), at *www-cta.ornl.gov.* Sexual intercourse estimated on the basis of James Trussell et al., "The Economic Value of Contraception: A Comparison of 15 Methods," *American Journal of Public Health,* April 1995.

23. *Linking Tax Law and Sustainable Urban Development: The Taxpayer Relief Act of 1997* (Washington, DC: Environmental Law Institute, 1998).

24. The Lovinses have used this metaphor in many of their works, but they credit it to their friend, aikido master and business consultant Tom Crum. For more on aikido politics, see the Web site of the Rocky Mountain Institute in Snowmass, Colorado, *www.rmi.org.*

25. Stevens, op. cit. note 4.

26. Density thresholds and driving patterns from Peter W. G. Newman and Jeffrey R. Kenworthy, *Cities and Automobile Dependence* (Brookfield, Vt.: Grower Technical, 1989). For a fuller discussion of urban design and transportation, see Alan Thein Durning, *The Car and the City* (Seattle: NEW, 1996).

27. Portland's density calculated from *1990 Census of Population and Housing* on CD-ROM (Washington, DC: US Census Bureau, 1992). Seattle from *Population and Housing Estimates, 1993 and*

1994 (Seattle: Puget Sound Regional Council [PSRC], 1995). Vancouver from *Profile of Census Tracts in Matsqui and Vancouver,* Part A (Ottawa: StatCan, 1992).

28. Suburban-urban driving from John Holtzclaw, "Using Residential Patterns and Transit to Decrease Auto Dependence and Costs," Natural Resources Defense Council, San Francisco, 1994. Bus frequency and self-sufficiency from Preston Schiller and Jeffrey R. Kenworthy, "Prospects for Sustainable Transportation in the Pacific Northwest, " unpublished manuscript, Feb. 1996.

29. "Puget Sound Housing Preference Study," prepared for PSRC by Decision Data, Kirkland, Washington, 1994.

30. Decreased driving from 1,000 Friends of Oregon, newsletters and reports, Portland, 1993–95.

31. Seattle sidewalks from Schiller and Kenworthy, op. cit. note 28. Trip length from Patricia S. Hu and Jennifer Young, *National Personal Transportation Survey: NPTS Databook 1990* (Washington, DC: FHWA, 1993), at *www-cta.ornl.gov/npts/1990*. Benefits of bike lanes from *The Environmental Benefits of Bicycling and Walking* (Washington, DC: FHWA, 1993).

32. Traffic calming benefits from Todd Litman, "Traffic Calming Benefits, Costs and Equity Impacts," Victoria Transport Policy Institute (VTPI), Victoria, 1999. Seattle success and international examples from Reid Ewing, *Traffic Calming: State of the Practice* (Washington, DC: Institute of Transportation Engineers, 1999).

33. History of least-cost planning from "Least-Cost Planning: Principles, Applications, and Issues," prepared for FHWA, Office of the Environment and Planning by ECONorthwest, Eugene; and Parsons, Brinckerhoff, Quade and Douglas, Portland; July 1995. Description of least-cost planning from David Reinke and Daniel Malarkey, "Implementing Integrated Transportation Planning in Metropolitan Planning Organization: Procedural and Analytical Issues," *Transportation Research Record,* 1996.

34. Success of least-cost planning from Edward W. Sheets and Richard H. Watson, "Least-Cost Transportation Planning: Lessons from the Northwest Power Planning Council," Institute for Public Policy and Management, University of Washington, Seattle, Jan. 1994. Electricity growth rates from Terry Morlan, Northwest Power Planning Council, Portland, private communication, Nov. 7, 2000.

35. Best buys for Seattle from Dick Nelson and Don Shakow, "Least-Cost Planning: A Tool for Metropolitan Transportation Decision

Making," *Transportation Research Record,* 1995; and Emory Bundy, "Why Rail?" *Open Spaces,* summer 2000.

36. Curitiba from Jonas Rabinovitch and Josef Leitman, "Urban Planning in Curitiba," *Scientific American,* March 1996. Portland signals from Willie Rotich, Portland Bureau of Transportation, private communication, Nov. 8 and 15, 2000. Eugene transit from Lane Transit District, "Bus Rapid Transit," *www.ltd.org/brt1.html,* March 5, 2001. Seattle from Kery Murakami, "Schell Presents His Neighborhood Transit Blueprint," *Seattle Post-Intelligencer,* Jan. 31, 2001. King County from Chris McGann, "Vanpool Cruising on Road to Success," *Seattle Post-Intelligencer,* March 27, 2000.

37. Robert W. Behnke, "Minerva: A Smart Jitney, Smart Community System for Residents of Rural, Suburban, and Urban Areas," presented at Oregon Mayors Association Conference, July 1999; and Robert W. Behnke, consultant, Beaverton, Oregon, private communication, fall 2000.

38. "Protect the best, restore the rest" is the motto of the Pacific Rivers Council, a watershed conservation organization in Eugene; see Bob Doppelt et al., *Entering the Watershed* (Washington, DC: Island Press, 1993) for the science behind its strategy.

39. Wilds from Michael E. Soulé and John Terborgh, eds., *Continental Conservation: Scientific Foundations of Regional Reserve Networks* (Washington, DC: Island Press, 1999). Services value from Keri Konarska and Paul Sutton, Dept. of Geography, University of Denver, private communication, Dec. 8, 2000; and Ernie Niemi and Anne Fifield, "Seeing the Forests for Their Green: Economic Benefits of Forest Protection, Recreation and Restoration," prepared for the Sierra Club by ECONorthwest, Eugene, Aug. 2000.

40. NCEAS Working Group on Marine Reserves, "Scientific Consensus Statement on Marine Reserves and Marine Protected Areas," National Center for Ecological Analysis and Synthesis (NCEAS), University of California, Santa Barbara, *www.nceas.ucsb.edu,* March 1, 2001; and Callum M. Roberts, "Guides to Implementing Successful Reserves," paper presented at the American Association for the Advancement of Science annual meeting, San Francisco, Feb. 17, 2001, at *www.compassline.org/frame.html,* March 1, 2001.

41. BC protected area from BC MELP, "Protected Areas Indicator," *www.elp.gov.bc.ca/sppl/soerpt,* Dec. 26, 2000. National monuments in Northwest from Douglas Jehl, "Clinton vs. Western In-

terests Encapsuled in Battle over Missouri River," *New York Times,* Sept. 14, 2000. Roadless areas initiative from US Forest Service (USFS), "Roadless Area Conservation, Final Rule," *Federal Register,* Jan. 12, 2001, at *roadless.fs.fed.us.* Loomis Forest protection from Mitch Friedman and Dan Hagen, "We Are Not Alone: A Case Study in Public Support for Biodiversity Conservation," *Society for Conservation Biology Newsletter,* Nov. 2000. New BC park from Joel Connelly, "BC to Create Vast New Park on Border," *Seattle Post-Intelligencer,* Jan. 17, 2001. Off-limits share based on Ryan, op. cit. note 3.

42. National Marine Sanctuaries, "Come Explore Our Nation's Deepest Treasures," *www.sanctuaries.nos.noaa.gov,* Feb. 25, 2001; and BC Land Use Coordination Office, "Marine Protected Areas: A Strategy for Canada's Pacific Coast," Aug. 1998 discussion paper, *www.luco.gov.bc.ca/pas/mpa/dispap.htm,* Feb. 25, 2001.

43. Oregon watersheds and anchor habitats from Mark G. Henjum et al., *Interim Protection for Late-Successional Forests, Fisheries, and Watersheds: National Forests East of the Cascade Crest, Oregon and Washington* (Bethesda, Md.: Wildlife Society, 1994); and "A Salmon Conservation Strategy for the Tillamook and Clatsop State Forests," Ecotrust, Oregon Trout, and Wild Salmon Center, Portland, 2000. Cascades and Willapa from Cascades Conservation Partnership, *www.ecosystem.org/tccp,* Jan. 8, 2001; Lynda V. Mapes, "Conservancy Aims to Buy Watershed in Willapa Hills," *Seattle Times,* Sept. 27, 2000; and Pamela McAllister, "Ellsworth Creek," *Washington Wildlands,* fall 2000–winter 2001.

44. Ecosystem services from Robert Costanza et al., "The Value of the World's Ecosystem Services and Natural Capital," *Nature,* May 15, 1997; and Konarska and Sutton, op. cit. note 39.

45. *Aquatic Habitat Evaluation and Management Report* (Olympia: Public Works Dept., 1999); and Denny Creek Neighborhood Alliance, *www.dennycreek.com,* Feb. 8, 2001.

46. Alex McLean, "Clearing the Smoke," *Northwest Conservation,* winter 2000; Ross W. Gorte, "Timber Harvesting and Forest Fires," Congressional Research Service report, Aug. 22, 2000, at *www.cnie.org;* Thomas Michael Power, "Fire a Danger in Clearcuts Too," *Seattle Post-Intelligencer,* Aug. 20, 2000; Peter H. Morrison et al., *Assessment of Summer 2000 Wildfires: Landscape History, Current Condition and Ownership* (Winthrop, Wash.: Pacific Biodiversity Institute, 2000); Robert McClure, "Let

Some Lands Burn, Report Says," *Seattle Post-Intelligencer,* Sept. 5, 2000; and John S. MacNeil, "Forest Fire Plan Kindles Debate," *Science,* Sept. 1, 2000.

47. David Axelrod, "The Dimensions of Hope," *Chronicle of Community,* fall 2000.

48. Stevens, op. cit. note 4; and "Aikido FAQ," *www.aikidofaq.com,* Nov. 15, 2000.

49. Ernst von Weizsäcker et al., *Factor Four: Doubling Wealth, Halving Resource Use* (London: Earthscan, 1997).

50. SO_2 emission reductions and cleanup costs from US EPA, "Progress Report on the EPA Acid Rain Program," *www.epa.gov/airmarkets/progress/arpreport,* Jan. 4, 2001.

51. Rights exceeding rivers from Paul G. Risser et al., *Oregon State of the Environment Report 2000* (Salem: Oregon Progress Board, 2000). Protected river miles from Debbie DeRose, Oregon Water Trust, Portland, private communication, Oct. 4, 2000.

52. Grazing reform from Andy Kerr, "The Voluntary Retirement Option for Federal Public Land Grazing Permittees," *Rangelands,* Oct. 1998. Value of permits from Mark Salvo, American Lands Alliance, Portland, private communication, Jan. 9, 2001.

53. Idaho Watershed Project (IWP) from "Victory!!!" posted Jan. 12, 2000, and "Idaho Watersheds Project Wins Auction for 5,050 Acre Grazing Lease in Cassia County in Southern Idaho," posted Oct. 3, 2000, IWP e-mail archive list, at *www.idahowatersheds.org.* Grazing reprieves update from Dan Gallagher, "Board Takes Land Lease Away from High Bidder," *Idaho Statesman,* Dec. 13, 2000. Bonneville Power Administration grazing lease from "BPA Funds Idaho Grazing Acquisition to Protect Fish," *Watershed Messenger* (IWP), summer 2000, at *www.idahowatersheds.org.*

54. Pacific Forest Trust from Alan Thein Durning, *Green-Collar Jobs* (Seattle: NEW, 1999). Oregon Climate Trust from Sam Sadler, Oregon Office of Energy, Salem, private communication, Sept. 20, 2000; and Oregon Climate Trust, "Background," *www.climatetrust.org,* Nov. 7, 2000. Victoria program from Greenhouse Gas Emission Reduction Trading Pilot, "Offers and Trades," *www.gert.org,* Nov. 7, 2000. Climate Partners information from Climate Partners, "Climate Partners Offsets," *www.climatepartners.com,* Nov. 7, 2000.

55. Canada from *Pacific Region Integrated Fisheries Management Plan: Halibut 2000* (Vancouver, BC: Fisheries and Oceans Canada,

2000). Alaska from International Pacific Halibut Commission "Fishery History," *www.iphc.washington.edu,* Nov. 15, 2000.

56. Transfer of development rights from Neil Modie, "High-rises in Denny Triangle OK'd," *Seattle Post-Intelligencer,* April 11, 2000. Green power from Bonneville Environmental Foundation, "About BEF," *www.bonenvfdn.org,* Nov. 15, 2000.

57. Free parking spaces and daily driving per capita from Durning,. op. cit. note 26; US Census Bureau, op. cit. note 1; and StatCan, op. cit. note 1. Full cost of parking in 2000 estimated on the basis of average cost of parking per mile driven from Todd Litman, "Transportation Cost Analysis," VTPI, Victoria, 1995. Shares of parking bill from Todd Litman, "Marginalizing and Internalizing Parking and Insurance Costs to Achieve TDM Goals," prepared for NEW by VTPI, Victoria, Oct. 1995.

58. Regional parking requirements from Durning, op. cit. note 26. Effect on density from Clifford W. Cobb, *The Roads Aren't Free: Estimating the Full Social Cost of Driving and the Effects of Accurate Pricing* (San Francisco: Redefining Progress, 1998).

59. Portland from *Citywide Parking Ratios Project* (Portland: Bureau of Planning, 2000). Olympia from *Downtown Olympia Parking Management Strategy: Update Study* (Olympia: Public Works Dept., 1998). BC from Gordon Price, City Council, Vancouver, BC, private communication, Nov. 16, 2000.

60. Olympia from Andy Haub, Public Works Dept., Olympia, private communication, Nov. 16, 2000. Missoula from Steve King, Public Works Dept., Missoula, private communication, Nov. 27, 2000. Eugene from *City of Eugene Arterial Collector Street Plan* (Eugene: Planning and Development Dept., 1999). Kirkland from Rob Jammerman, Public Works Dept., Kirkland, Washington, private communication, Jan. 5, 2001.

61. Canadian law and enforcement from John C. Ryan, *Hazardous Handouts* (Seattle: NEW, 1995). United States law from the US EPA, "Tax Treatment of Employer-Provided Commute Benefits Summary," *www.epa.gov/oms/transp/comchoic/ccweb.htm,* Nov. 3, 2000.

62. California results from Todd Litman, "Internalizing and Marginalizing Parking Costs as a Transportation Demand Management Measure," VTPI, Victoria, 1995. Federal support from Jemae Pope, Strategic Planning Office, Seattle, private communication, Nov. 8, 2000.

63. Average insurance cost per mile from Todd Litman, "Marginalizing Insurance Costs as a Transportation Demand Management Measure," VTPI, Victoria, 1995; and Todd Litman, VTPI, Victoria, private communication, Jan. 5, 2001. Undercharging in British Columbia from Todd Litman, "Mileage-based Vehicle Insurance: Feasibility, Costs, and Benefits," VTPI, Victoria, Oct. 12, 2000.

64. Autograph program from Anne Eisenberg, "Paying for Car Insurance by the Mile," New York Times, April 20, 2000; and Progressive Insurance, "Progressive Testing New Product That Features Revolutionary Auto Insurance Rating Method," press release, www1.progressive.com, Oct. 12, 2000. National rollout from Maria Henderson, Progressive Insurance, Tallahassee, Florida, private communication, Dec. 19, 2000.

65. Insurance by the mile from Todd Litman, VTPI, Victoria; Paul Horton, Climate Solutions, Olympia; and Douglas Howell, Environmental and Energy Study Institute, Seattle, private communication, Oct. 2000.

66. Todd Litman et al., "Road Relief," Energy Outreach Center (now Climate Solutions), Olympia, 1998.

67. Driving reduction from Daniel Sperling et al., "Carsharing and Mobility Services: An Updated Overview," prepared for the Workshop on Managing Car Use for Sustainable Urban Travel, European Conference of Ministers of Transport/Organization for Economic Cooperation and Development, Dublin, Ireland, Dec. 1999, at www.calstart.org/resources/papers.

68. Northwesterners in BC, Oregon, and California calculated from US Census Bureau, op. cit. note 1; StatCan, op. cit. note 1; and California Dept. of Finance, "Reports and Research Papers: County Population Projections," www.dof.ca.gov, Nov. 2, 2000.

69. Bette K. Fishbein, Germany, Garbage, and the Green Dot: Challenging the Throwaway Society (New York: Inform, 1994).

70. Packaging consumption from Karl-Josef Baum, "Packaging in Distribution," paper presented at the Eighth Dresden Packaging Congress, Dresden, Germany, Dec. 1998. Durable crates and countries requiring take-backs from Gary Gardner and Payal Sampat, Mind over Matter: Recasting the Role of Materials in Our Lives (Washington, DC: Worldwatch Institute, 1998).

71. BC take-back rates from BC MELP, "Overview of Industry Product Stewardship in British Columbia," www.env.gov.bc.ca/epd/epdpa/ips, Sept. 28, 2000. Oregon recycling from Peter Spendelow,

Oregon Dept. of Environmental Quality (DEQ), Portland, private communication, Sept. 21, 2000. Seattle recycling from Jenny Bagby, Seattle Public Utilities, Seattle, private communication, Oct. 10, 2000; and "Summary of Recycling Program Impacts," Resource Planning Division, Seattle Public Utilities, 1995.

72. BC return rate from "Recovery Rates, Diversion Numbers," *Forum* (Encorp Pacific), Sept. 2000, at *www.encorpinc.com*. King County from King County Solid Waste Division, "Computer Recovery Project," *dnr.metrokc.gov,* Jan. 4, 2001. Oregon from Abby Boudouris, Oregon DEQ, Portland, private communication, Sept. 25, 2000. European product stewardship from Carola Hanisch, "Is Extended Producer Responsibility Effective?" *Environmental Science and Technology,* April 1, 2000.

73. Xerox Corporation, "Environment, Health, and Safety 2000 Progress Report," *www2.xerox.com/go/xrx/about_xerox/T_ehs.jsp,* Oct. 17, 2000; and Herman Miller, "About Us: Environment," *www.hermanmiller.com/us,* Dec. 12, 2000. Interface from Paul Hawken et al., *Natural Capitalism* (New York: Little Brown, 1999).

74. Stevens, op. cit. note 4. Morihei quoted in John Stevens and Walther V. Krenner, *Training with the Master: Lessons with Morihei Ueshiba, Founder of Aikido* (Boston: Shambhala, 1999).

75. For a fuller discussion of environmentally harmful subsidies, see Ryan, op. cit. note 61.

76. *State of Oregon 1997–99 Tax Expenditure Report* (Salem: Oregon Budget and Management Division, 1997); and *Tax Exemptions 1996* (Olympia: Washington Dept. of Revenue, 1995).

77. Columbia River salmon subsidies from Ryan, op. cit. note 61.

78. California, Idaho, Montana, Oregon, and Washington dedicate fuel tax revenue to roadwork; California also dedicates all sales tax on fuel sales to roadwork. Alaska and British Columbia are the only Northwest jurisdictions that do not earmark fuel tax revenue for roads, yet they spend more on roadwork than fuel taxes bring in. See Alan Thein Durning and Yoram Bauman, *Tax Shift* (Seattle: NEW, 1998).

79. US data from *Highway Statistics 1999,* op. cit. note 22. Seattle subsidy from "The Cost of Transportation: Expenditures on Surface Transportation in the Central Puget Sound Region for 1995 (Paper 1)," PSRC, Seattle, Oct. 1996. Regional subsidy based on Stanley I. Hart and Alvin L. Spivak, *Automobile Dependence and Denial: The Elephant in the Bedroom* (Pasadena, Calif.: New

Paradigm Books, 1993); and James J. MacKenzie et al., *The Going Rate: What It Really Costs to Drive* (Washington, DC: WRI, 1992). Washington from *Tax Exemptions 1996,* op. cit. note 76.

80. Vacation homes from Carlyn E. Orians and Marina Skumanich, "The Population-Environment Connection: What Does It Mean for Environmental Policy?" Battelle Seattle Research Center, Dec. 1995.

81. Alan Thein Durning and Christopher D. Crowther, *Misplaced Blame* (Seattle: NEW, 1997).

82. Oregon from Eben Fodor, "The Cost of Growth in Washington State," prepared for Columbia Public Interest Policy Institute by Fodor and Associates, Eugene, Oct. 2000; and "Growth and Its Impact in Oregon," Governor Kitzhaber's Task Force on Growth in Oregon, Salem, Jan. 1999. Washington from Patrick Mazza and Eben Fodor, "Taking Its Toll: The Hidden Costs of Sprawl in Washington State," Climate Solutions, Olympia, Feb. 2000, at *www.climatesolutions.org.*

83. Durning, op. cit. note 26.

84. US flood insurance from American Rivers, "Corps Reform: Flood Damage Reduction," *www.amrivers.org,* Jan. 22, 2001. Northwest fire-fighting spending from "Impacts of This Season's Wildfires," *Idaho Statesman,* Oct. 29, 2000; USFS Northern Rockies Coordination Center, "Northern Rockies Statistics 2000," *www.fs.fed.us/r1/fire/nrcc,* Jan. 30, 2001; and USFS National Interagency Fire Center, "Wildfire Season 2000 at a Glance," *www.nifc.gov/information.html.* Spending to protect private buildings from USFS, "Federal Wildland Fire Policy: Wildland/Urban Interface Protection," *www.fs.fed.us/land,* Dec. 18, 2000; and Rocky Barker, "Homeowners Could Help Stop Wildfires," *Idaho Statesman,* Sept. 30, 2000.

85. Value of housing tax breaks and housing assistance comparison from US Congress, Joint Committee on Taxation, *Estimates of Federal Tax Expenditures for Fiscal Years 2000–2004* (Washington, DC: US Government Printing Office, 1999), at *www.house.gov/jct/s-13-99.pdf.* Low-income housing spending from Jason DeParle, "Slamming the Door," *New York Times Magazine,* Oct. 20, 1996. Oregon tax breaks from *State of Oregon 1997–99 Tax Expenditure Report,* op. cit. note 76.

86. Canadian property tax from *1996 British Columbia Financial and Economic Review* (Victoria: BC Ministry of Finance and Corpo-

rate Relations [BC MFCR], 1996); and *Government of Canada Tax Expenditures 1997* (Ottawa: Dept. of Finance, 1997).

87. Tax credit calculated by dividing the 1999 value of real estate tax deductions and mortgage interest tax deductions by the total number of income tax returns claiming those deductions, from US Congress, op. cit. note 85.

88. Public land percentage from *Canada Yearbook 1994* (Ottawa: StatCan, 1994); *State of the Environment Report for British Columbia* (Victoria and North Vancouver: BC MELP and Environment Canada, 1993); Philip L. Jackson and A. Jon Kimerling, eds., *Atlas of the Pacific Northwest*, 8th ed. (Corvallis: Oregon State Univ. Press, 1993); *County and City Data Book, 1994* (Washington, DC: US Census Bureau, 1994); *Land Area of the National Forest System* (Washington, DC: USFS, 1992); Rick Griffen, USFS, Juneau, private communication, June 8, 1994; and Randy Hagenstein, Pacific GIS, Anchorage, private communication, March 10, 1995.

89. Irrigators' water use from Solley et al., op. cit. note 10. Costs from US Bureau of Reclamation from US House Committee on Natural Resources, Subcommittee on Oversight and Investigations, *Taxing from the Taxpayer: Public Subsidies for Natural Resource Development* (Washington, DC: US Government Printing Office, 1994). Northwest rivers from Charles F. Wilkinson, *Crossing the Next Meridian: Land, Water, and the Future of the West* (Washington, DC: Island Press, 1992). Columbia Basin from Columbia Basin Institute, "Water Conservation for In-stream Recapture on the Bureau of Reclamation's Columbia Basin Project: Opportunities and Obstacles," testimony submitted to US House Committee on Natural Resources, Subcommittee on Oversight and Investigations, Washington, DC, July 19, 1994.

90. US royalties from Thomas J. Hilliard et al., *Golden Patents, Empty Pockets* (Washington, DC: Mineral Policy Center, 1994); US House Committee on Natural Resources, Subcommittee on Oversight and Investigations, op. cit. note 89; and Wilkinson, op. cit. note 89.

91. BC timber subsidies from Robert Gale et al., "Accounting for the Forests: A Methodological Critique of Price Waterhouse's Report, *The Forest Industry in British Columbia 1997*," Ecological Economics, Victoria, May 1999. Northwest states' timber subsidies from the Wilderness Society, "Commercial Timber Sale on National Forests, by Forest, FY1997," *www.wildernesss.org/own/timbersales_1997.htm*, Nov. 20, 2000.

92. John Stevens, *Aikido: The Way of Harmony* (Boston: Shambhala, 1984); "The Aikido Primer," *home.neo.lrun.com/sotnak/primer.html*, Nov. 15, 2000; and Stevens, op. cit. note 4.
93. Northwest growth rate from US Census Bureau, op. cit. note 1; StatCan, op. cit. note 1; and *Annual Demographic Statistics,* cat. no. 91-213 (Ottawa: StatCan, 1994). Third World population growth, 1995–2000, from United Nations Statistical Division, "Indicators of Population," *www.un.org/Depts/unsd,* Jan. 3, 2001.
94. Migration from sources in note 93. Natural increase over time from Durning and Crowther, op. cit. note 81.
95. See Durning and Crowther, op. cit. note 81, for fuller discussion of these ideas.
96. Total fertility rates from *British Columbia Population Forecast Update* (Victoria: BC MFCR, 1996); *1995 Population Trends for Washington State* (Olympia: Washington Office of Financial Management, 1995); *Oregon Vital Statistics Annual Report 1994* (Salem: Oregon Dept. of Human Services, 1996); and Center for Vital Statistics and Health Policy, Idaho Dept. of Health and Welfare, Boise, private communication, June 1997. Share of fertility due to poverty from Mike A. Males, School of Social Ecology, University of California, Irvine, data analysis for NEW, May 1997; and Amara Bachu, *Fertility of American Women: June 1992* (Washington, DC: US Census Bureau, 1993). Comparisons of Northwest fertility rates with those in low-poverty industrial countries from Lee Rainwater and Timothy M. Smeeding, "Doing Poorly: The Real Income of American Children in a Comparative Perspective," *Luxembourg Income Study* (Syracuse, NY: Syracuse Univ., 1995); and *1995* and *1996 World Population Data Sheet* (Washington, DC: Population Reference Bureau, 1995 and 1996). Ratio of childbearing by class estimated from Bachu and from T. J. Matthews and Stephanie J. Ventura, "Birth and Fertility Rates by Educational Attainment: United States, 1994," US National Center for Health Statistics, Hyattsville, Md., April 2, 1997.
97. Share of teen mothers who are poor from *Sex and America's Teenagers* (New York: Alan Guttmacher Institute [AGI], 1994). Teen births as a share of total births and natural increase (births minus deaths) from Washington Dept. of Health, "Washington State Vital Statistics Overview," *www.doh.wa.gov/ehsphl/chs,* Jan. 17, 2001; Oregon Dept. of Human Services, "Oregon Vital Statistics Annual Report 1998," *www.ohd.hr.state.or.us/chs,* Jan. 17, 2001; Idaho Dept. of Health and Welfare, "Idaho Vital Statistics '98,"

www2.state.id.us/dhw/VS, Jan. 17, 2001; and BC Ministry of Health, "Selected Vital Statistics and Health Status Indicators, Annual Report 1998," *www.hlth.gov.bc.ca/vs,* Jan. 17, 2001. Relationship between income and childbearing from Kristin Luker, *Dubious Conceptions: The Politics of Teenage Pregnancy* (Cambridge, Mass.: Harvard Univ. Press, 1996).

98. California's guaranteed education from Dan Smith, "State to Aid Needy on College Cost," *Sacramento Bee,* Sept. 12, 2000.

99. Seniors lifted out of poverty from John L. Palmer et al., eds., *The Vulnerable* (Washington, DC: Urban Institute Press, 1988). Government spending on children and seniors from Congressional Budget Office, "Federal Spending on the Elderly and Children," *www.cbo.gov,* Jan. 3, 2001. State and local spending from the Concord Coalition, "Facing Facts: The Truth about Entitlements and the Budget," *www.concordcoalition.org,* Jan. 3, 2001.

100. Share of school-age mothers who have suffered abuse from M. Jocelyn Elders and Alexa E. Albert, "Adolescent Pregnancy and Sexual Abuse," *Journal of the American Medical Association,* Aug. 19, 1998. Share of all teen girls who have suffered abuse from Jason DeParle, "Early Sex Abuse Hinders Many Women on Welfare," *New York Times,* Nov. 28, 1999.

101. Debra Boyer et al., *Victimization and Other Risk Factors for Child Maltreatment among School-age Parents* (Seattle: Washington Alliance Concerned with School-Age Parents [now Advancing Solutions to Adolescent Pregnancy], 1992).

102. Debra Boyer et al., op. cit. note 101; and Andrea J. Sedlak and Diane D. Broadhurst, "Executive Summary of the Third National Incidence Study of Child Abuse and Neglect," National Center on Child Abuse and Neglect, US Dept. of Health and Human Services, Washington, DC, Sept. 1996.

103. Working conditions in child protection agencies from Riveland Associates, "Child Protective Services in Washington State Administrative Assessment," *www.dshs.wa.gov,* Oct. 18, 2000; and Richard N. Brandon et al., "Developing a Communication Strategy for Protecting Children," Human Services Policy Center, University of Washington, Seattle, Feb. 20, 1996. Percentage of abuse and neglect reports investigated in Washington from Carol Smith, "Major Overhaul Urged for CPS," *Seattle Post-Intelligencer,* Oct. 10, 2000. Underreporting of abuse from Sedlak and Broadhurst, op. cit. note 102.

104. Recommendations for sexual-abuse monitoring from David Finkelhor, "Improving Research, Policy, and Practice to Understand Child Sexual Abuse," *Journal of the American Medical Association,* Dec. 2, 1998. Washington's program from Diana English, Children's Administration, Washington Dept. of Social and Health Services (DSHS), Seattle, private communication, Jan. 10, 2001; and Cindy Ellingson, Children's Administration, DSHS, Olympia, private communication, Jan. 24, 2001. Washington's leadership role from David Finkelhor, Crimes against Children Research Center, Durham, New Hampshire, private communication, Dec. 31, 2000.

105. Chances of abuse and abduction from Sedlak and Broadhurst, op. cit. note 102; David Finkelhor et al., *Missing, Abducted, Runaway, and Throwaway Children in America* (Washington, DC: US Dept. of Justice, 1990); and Sandy K. Wurtele, "Another Look at Child-Focused Sexual Abuse Prevention Programs," *Prevention Update* (Committee for Children, Seattle), fall 1996.

106. Trend in births from unintended pregnancies from Stanley K. Henshaw, "Unintended Pregnancy in the United States," *Family Planning Perspectives,* Jan.–Feb. 1998. Share of births from unintended pregnancies from *PRAMS 1997 Surveillance Report* (Atlanta: US Centers for Disease Control and Prevention, 1999); and Institute of Medicine, *Best Intentions: Unintended Pregnancy and the Well-Being of Children and Families* (Washington, DC: National Academy Press, 1995).

107. Canadian unintended pregnancy rate from Institute of Medicine, op. cit. note 106. California law from Tamar Lewin, "Insurance Should Cover Cost of Contraceptives, Suit Says," *New York Times,* July 20, 2000.

108. Washington coverage from "Reproductive Health Benefits Survey," Office of the Insurance Commissioner, Olympia, 1998. Viagra coverage from Amy Goldstein, "Viagra's Success Fuels Gender-Bias Debate: Birth Control Advocates Raise Issue," *Washington Post,* May 20, 1998. Cost-effectiveness from James Trussell et al., op. cit. note 22.

109. Seattle lawsuit from Lewin, op. cit. note 107, and Ruth Schubert, "Pharmacist Sues, Wants Employer to Cover Birth Control," *Seattle Post-Intelligencer,* July 20, 2000. EEOC ruling from Tamar Lewin, "In Anti-bias Ruling, Panel Finds Health Plans Should Cover the Pill," *New York Times,* Dec. 15, 2000. Washington

ruling from Tyrone Beason, "Senn Tells Health Insurers to Pay for Contraceptives," *Seattle Union Record,* Jan. 5, 2001. Cost of medicine from *Woman's Health Insurance Costs and Experiences* (New York: Women's Research and Education Institute, 1994).

110. Washington uninsured rate from Wei Yen, "Health Insurance Coverage of Washington's Non-elderly Population," Washington State Population Survey, Research Brief 6, Washington State Office of Financial Management, Olympia, 1999, at *www.ofm.wa.gov/sps/briefs/brief6.pdf.* Prevented pregnancies from Jacqueline Darroch Forrest and Renee Samara, "Impact of Publicly Funded Contraceptive Services on Unintended Pregnancies and Implications for Medicaid Expenditures," *Family Planning Perspectives,* Sept.–Oct. 1996. Federal support from *Fulfilling the Promise* (New York: AGI, 2000). Washington women from Community and Family Health, *Benefit:Cost Analysis of Family Planning in Washington State* (Olympia: Washington Dept. of Health, 1994).

111. Sexual intercourse derived using population figures and the reported frequency that women aged 15–44 have sex from Trussell et al., op. cit. note 22; US Census Bureau, op. cit. note 1; StatCan, op. cit. note 1; and *Statistical Abstract of the United States 1999* (Washington, DC: US Census Bureau, 1999). Couples who forgo contraceptives estimated from J. Abma et al., "Fertility, Family Planning, and Women's Health: New Data from the 1995 National Survey of Family Growth," *Vital and Health Statistics,* May 1997. Condom failure estimated from J. Trussell et al., "The Essentials of Contraception: Safety, Effectiveness, and Personal Consideration," in R. A. Hatcher et al., *Contraceptive Technology,* 17th revised ed. (New York: Irvington, 1998). Resulting pregnancies estimated from J. Trussell et al., "The Effectiveness of the Yuzpe Regimen of Emergency Contraception," *Family Planning Perspectives,* March–April 1996. Washington program from Nancy Montgomery, "Morning-After Project a Success," *Seattle Times,* July 25, 1999.

112. Montgomery, op. cit. note 111.

113. Program for Alternative Technologies in Health (PATH), "Emergency Contraception Collaborative Agreement Pilot Project," *www.path.org,* Aug. 14, 2000.

114. Prescriptions from PATH, op. cit. note 113. Chain-pharmacy prescription increase from Elisa S. Wells et al., "Using Pharmacies in Washington State to Expand Access to Emergency Contraception,"

Family Planning Perspectives, Nov.–Dec. 1998. Prevented pregnancies from PATH and Wells et al.

115. Project expansion from PATH, "Eastern Washington ECP Access Project," *www.path.org,* Oct. 12, 2000; Gina Kolata, "Without Fanfare, Morning-After Pill Gets a Closer Look," *New York Times,* Oct. 8, 2000; Jane E. Boggess, Public Health Institute, Berkeley, private communication, Nov. 1, 2000; and Judith Chrystal, British Columbia Pharmacy Association, Richmond, private communication, Sept. 15, 2000. Number of Wal-Mart stores from Amy Wyatt, Wal-Mart, Bentonville, Arkansas, private communication, Oct. 15, 2000.

116. British Columbia trials from Graeme Smith, "Doctors to Test French Abortion Pill Here," *Toronto Star,* July 7, 2000.

117. Mifepristone history from Margaret Talbot, "The Little White Bombshell," *New York Times Magazine,* July 11, 2000; and Gina Kolata, "Drug Offers More Privacy, and Could Reshape Debate," *New York Times,* Sept. 29, 2000. Women's reactions to mifepristone from Beverly Winikoff et al., "Acceptability and Feasibility of Early Pregnancy Termination by Mifepristone-Misoprostol," *Archives of Family Medicine,* July–Aug. 1998.

118. Stevens, op. cit. note 4.

119. For a fuller discussion of tax shifting, see Durning and Bauman, op. cit. note 78.

120. Number of European tax shifts from Lester R. Brown et al., *Vital Signs 2000* (New York: Norton, 2000).

121. "Taxes for a Cleaner Planet," *Economist,* June 28, 1997. Economists and Nobel laureates from Redefining Progress, "The Economists' Statement on Climate Change," *www.rprogress.org,* Jan. 18, 2001. Oregon bill from Sarah Doll, Oregon Environmental Council (OEC), Portland, private communication, Jan. 31, 2001; and OEC, "Pesticide Program," *www.orcouncil.org,* Feb. 7, 2001. BC initiative from Paul Ramsey, "Environmental Initiatives Part 1: Tax Shift Update and Status Report," in *Budget 2000* (Victoria: BC MFCR, 2000), at *www.bcbudget.gov.bc.ca,* Jan. 10, 2000.

122. Pollution and health impacts from Durning and Bauman, op. cit. note 78, and references therein. Fossil fuel–derived CO_2 emissions based on energy consumption data in EIA, "State Energy Data Report 1997," *www.eia.doe.gov,* Oct. 20, 2000.

123. Washington from *Tax Reference Manual* (Olympia: Dept. of Revenue, 1999), at *www.dor.wa.gov/reports/taxref99.* California pes-

ticide tracking from William Pease et al., *Pesticide Use in California: Strategies for Reducing Environmental Health Impacts* (Berkeley: California Policy Seminar, 1996). Oregon pesticide tracking from OEC, op. cit. note 121.

124. Pollution taxes from Durning and Bauman, op. cit. note 78.
125. Vehicle pollution tax calculations from Durning and Bauman, op. cit. note 78. Carbon tax calculations from Ryan, op. cit. note 10.
126. Hydropower taxes from Durning and Bauman, op. cit. note 78. Alaska revenues from *Spring 1996 Revenue Sources Book: Forecast and Historical Data* (Juneau: Alaska Dept. of Revenue, 1996), at *www.revenue.state.ak.us.*
127. US water consumption from Solley et al., op. cit. note 10. Idaho sales tax revenue from *Annual Report 1996* (Boise: Idaho State Tax Commission, 1997). Price comparisons estimated from Jeff Allen, "Liquid Assets: The Potential of Water Use Fees," draft paper prepared for Office of Research, California Senate, Sacramento, 1992. Price increase estimated from Durning and Bauman, op. cit. note 78.
128. Resource tax generation calculation from Durning and Bauman, op. cit. note 78. Washington's regressive tax system from Michael P. Ettlinger et al., *Who Pays? A Distributional Analysis of the Tax System in All 50 States* (Washington, DC: Citizens for Tax Justice and the Institution on Taxation and Economic Policy, 1996).
129. Durning and Bauman, op. cit. note 78.
130. Portland from *State of Oregon 1997–99 Tax Expenditure Report,* op. cit. note 76. Seattle from *Tax Exemptions 1998* (Olympia: Washington Dept. of Revenue, 1997); and Seattle Office of Housing, "Property Tax Exemption for Multifamily Housing," *www.cityofseattle.net/housing/loanprograms.htm,* March 12, 2001. Canadian land-value tax from Pam Neary, "International Experience with Land Value Taxes," *New Rules* (Institute for Local Self-Reliance, Minneapolis), summer 1999. Australia and Taiwan from Thomas A. Gihring, "Incentive Property Taxation in Vancouver, Washington," Public Finance Research Center, Olympia, Nov. 1996. Pennsylvania from Wallace E. Oates and Robert M. Schwab, "The Impact of Urban Land Taxation: The Pittsburgh Experience," *National Tax Journal,* March 1997.
131. Washington counties tax shift study from Gihring, op. cit. note 130; and "Converting from a Single Rate to a Differential Rate Property Tax; Resulting Changes in Tax Burden among Land Use

Classes in King County, Washington," paper presented at the Pacific Northwest Regional Economic Conference, Seattle, April 28–30, 1994. Oregon from Tom Gihring and Kris Nelson, "Tax Shift Sequential to a Land-based Property Tax System in Salem, Oregon," unpublished manuscript, Seattle, Nov. 1999.

132. Toll generation from Durning and Bauman, op. cit. note 78, and Aubrey Davis et al., "Summary: Transportation Pricing Discussions, European Visit, Sept. 2000," PSRC, Seattle, Oct. 18, 2000. Congestion time and gasoline costs from David L. Shrank and Timothy J. Lomax, *Urban Roadway Congestion, 1982 to 1994* (College Station: Texas Transportation Institute, 1997).

133. Variable toll acceptance from Edward Sullivan, "Evaluating the Impacts of the SR 91 Variable-Toll Express Lane Facility," final report prepared for State of California Dept. of Transportation by Applied Research and Development Facility, California Polytechnic State University, May 1998, at *gridlock.calpoly.edu/~esulliva/sr91/final_rpt/finalrep.pdf*.

134. Portland airport from Bill Stewart, "Study Suggests Tolls Instead of Gas Tax," *Oregonian*, Dec. 25, 2000. San Diego and Houston from C. Kenneth Orski, *Innovation Briefs*, Nov.–Dec. 1998 and July–Aug. 1998.

135. Tacoma bridge tolls from Bruce Ramsey, "As Traffic Worsens, Economic Reality Could Take Its Toll," *Seattle Post-Intelligencer*, March 10, 1999. Oregon congestion pricing developments from Bridget Wieghart, Metropolitan Service Council, Portland, private communication, Jan. 25, 2001. TransLink tolling initiative from Ken Dobbell, "Strategic Transportation Plan Funding Options: Recommendation," memo to Greater Vancouver Transportation Authority Board of Directors, Vancouver, BC, Oct. 18, 2000; and Ray Straatsma, Better Environmentally Sound Transportation, Vancouver, BC, private communication, Jan. 31, 2001.

136. "1995 Metropolitan Transportation Plan," PSRC, Seattle, 1995; and "Regional Transportation System Action Strategy: Six-Year Action Strategy," PSRC, Seattle, Jan. 1998.

137. Median lifespan of a new truck from *Transportation Energy Data Book*, op. cit. note 22.

138. California feebates from Michael Totten and Nita Settina, *Energy-Wise Options for State and Local Governments*, 2d ed. (Washington, DC: Center for Policy Alternatives, 1993). Maryland, Ontario, and additional California information from Kelly

Hill, "Feebates," *State Legislative Report,* National Conference of State Legislatures, Jan. 1997.

139. Payback gap from Christopher Flavin and Alan B. Durning, *Building on Success: The Age of Energy Efficiency* (Washington, DC: Worldwatch Institute, 1988). The effectiveness of a nationwide feebate derived from Kenneth E. Train et al., "Fees and Rebates on New Vehicles: Impacts on Fuel Efficiency, Carbon Dioxide Emissions, and Consumer Surplus," *Transportation Research E: Logistics and Transportation Review,* March 1997.

140. Oregon feebate from Oregon Office of Energy, "Report on Reducing Oregon's Greenhouse Gas Emissions," *www.energy.state.or.us/climate/gggas.htm,* Sept. 13, 2000. British Columbia from Dan Perrin, "Options to Reduce Light-Duty Vehicle Emissions in British Columbia: Final Report," prepared for BC MFCR by Perrin, Thorau and Associates, Oct. 20, 2000.

141. Stevens, op. cit. note 4.

142. US toxic releases from US EPA, "Toxic Release Inventory Explorer," op. cit. note 16. Economic growth from BEA, op. cit. note 1, Oct. 24, 2000. British Columbia releases from Environment Canada, op. cit. note 16.

143. Monitored chemicals as fraction of all chemicals from *Toxic Chemicals: EPA's Toxic Release Inventory Is Useful but Can Be Improved* (Washington, DC: General Accounting Office, 1991). Chemicals covered by US law from US EPA, "Toxic Release Inventory Explorer," op. cit. note 16. Chemicals covered by Canadian law from Environment Canada, "National Pollutant Release Inventory: About the NPRI 1998, *www.ec.gc.ca/pdb/npri,* Oct. 21, 2000. Waste reclassification from Thomas E. Natan Jr., and Catherine G. Miller, "Are Toxic Release Inventory Reductions Real?" *Environmental Science and Technology,* Aug. 1, 1998.

144. "2000 Hazardous Substance Tracking Instructions," Eugene Fire Prevention Bureau, 2000; and Mary O'Brien, risk assessment consultant, Eugene, private communication, Jan. 25, 2001.

145. US EPA, "National Air Pollution Emissions Trends Update, 1970–1997," op. cit. note 16.

146. Dar Crammond, "Water Use Measurement and Reporting," *Big River News,* fall 2000; and Tom Geiger, "Protecting Water: Our Future Depends on It," *Washington Environmental Council Voices,* summer 2000.

147. Oregon pesticide tracking from OEC, op. cit. note 121. California from William Pease et al., op. cit. note 123.

148. Gordon Hamilton, "BC Logger Certified to Take Old-Growth Trees Despite Eco-Worries," *Vancouver Sun*, Sept. 14, 2000.

149. Home Depot pledge from Katie Sosnowchik, "Do-It-Yourself Green," *Green@Work*, March–April 2000. Market share from Cam Brewer, "Hanging in the Balance: Tough Questions for Certification," *Ecoforestry*, spring 2000.

150. Weyerhaeuser Company, "1999 Annual Environment, Health, and Safety Report," *www.weyerhaeuser.com*, Jan. 2, 2001.

151. Marine council and Unilever from Cathy R. Wessells et al., "Assessing Consumer Preferences for Ecolabeled Seafood: The Influence of Species, Certifier, and Household Attributes," *American Journal of Agricultural Economics*, Dec. 1999. Salmon certification from Margot Higgins, "Alaska Salmon Earn Landmark Seal of Approval," *Environmental News Network*, Sept. 7, 2000.

152. Seattle policy from Seattle Public Utilities, "Sustainable Building Policy," *www.cityofseattle.net/util/rescons*, Jan. 2, 2001. Portland policy from Brian J. Back, "City Leads by Example with Green Buildings Act," *Business Journal of Portland*, Jan. 15, 2001.

153. US Dept. of Energy, "Green Power Network," *www.eren.doe.gov/greenpower*, Jan. 2, 2001.

154. Sales growth from Organic Trade Association, "Business Facts," *www.ota.com*, July 25, 2000. US Food and Drug Administration standards from Marian Burrows, "US Imposes Standards for Organic Food Labeling," *New York Times*, Dec. 21, 2000.

155. James R. Karr and Ellen W. Chu, "Sustaining Living Rivers," *Hydrobiologia*, April 2000; and James R. Karr, "Rivers as Sentinels: Using the Biology of Rivers to Guide Landscape Management," in R. J. Naiman and R. E. Bilby, eds., *River Ecology and Management: Lessons from the Pacific Coastal Ecoregion* (New York: Springer, 1998).

156. James R. Karr and Ellen W. Chu, *Restoring Life in Running Waters: Better Biological Monitoring* (Washington, DC: Island Press, 1999); Randall E. Sanders, ed., *A Guide to Ohio Streams* (Columbus: Ohio Chapter of the American Fisheries Society, 2000); and Chris O. Yoder and Edward T. Rankin, "The Role of Biological Indicators in a State Water Quality Management Process," *Environmental Monitoring and Assessment*, June 1998.

157. Washington and Oregon from *2000 Washington State Water Quality Assessment* (Olympia: Washington Dept. of Ecology [DOE], 2000); and *Oregon's 2000 Water Quality Status Assessment Report* (Salem: Oregon DEQ, 2000).

158. US states from Leska Fore, Statistical Design, Seattle, private communication, Nov. 22, 2000; Wayne S. Davis et al., *Summary of State Biological Assessment Programs for Streams and Rivers* (Washington, DC: US EPA, 1996); US EPA, "State and Territory Summaries," *National Water Quality Inventory: 1998 Report to Congress, www.epa.gov/305b/98report/;* Jeff Hock and Drew Grant, Alaska Dept. of Environmental Conservation, private communications, Nov. and Dec. 2000; William H. Clark, *1998 Idaho Water Quality Status Report* (Boise: Idaho Division of Environmental Quality, 1998); Christopher A. Mebane, "Testing Bioassessment Metrics: Macroinvertebrate, Sculpin, and Salmonid Responses to Stream Habitat, Sediment, and Metals," *Environmental Monitoring and Assessment,* 2001, in press; Rick Hafele and Daria Mochan, Oregon DEQ, Portland, private communication, Jan. 8, 2001; Robert M. Hughes, Dynamac, Corvallis, private communication, Dec. 15, 2000; Robert M. Hughes et al., "A Process for Developing and Evaluating Indices of Fish Assemblage Integrity," *Canadian Journal of Fisheries and Aquatic Sciences,* July 1998; Paul G. Risser et al., op. cit. note 51; Bob Bukantis, Montana Dept. of Health and Environmental Science, Helena, private communication, Dec. 4, 2000; *Biological Assessment of Small Streams in the Coast Range Ecoregion and the Yakima River Basin* (Olympia: Washington DOE, 1999); Glenn Merritt and Robert Plotnikoff, Washington DOE, Olympia, private communication, Jan. 2, 2001. British Columbia from *Impact Assessment of River Ecosystems in the Skeena Region,* 1997 and 1998 reports on CD-ROM (Terrace, BC: Bio Logic Consulting, 1999); and *British Columbia Approved Water Quality Guidelines (Criteria)* (Victoria: BC MELP, 1998); *A Freshwater Strategy for British Columbia* (Victoria: BC MELP, 1999 and 2000 update).

159. Puget Sound biomonitoring from Karr, op. cit. note 155. Shrub-steppe biomonitoring from Diana N. Kimberling et al., "Measuring Human Disturbance Using Terrestrial Invertebrates in Shrub-Steppe of Eastern Washington (USA)," unpublished manuscript. Volunteers and students from Susan Gordon, "Larvae Collectors Measure Health of Water," *Tacoma News Tribune,* Oct. 11, 2000; Associated Press, "Yakima Students Create New Life in Wide Hollow Creek," *Olympian,* Nov. 7, 2000; and Leska Fore et al., "Assessing the Performance of Volunteers in Monitoring Streams," *Freshwater Biology,* 2001, in press.

160. Stevens, op. cit. note 4.

161. John Kitzhaber, "Executive Order No. EO-00-07," Office of the Governor, Salem, May 17, 2000.

162. Archimedes quoted in Pappus of Alexandria, "Collection," *Synagoge,* Book VIII, c. 340 A.D., at *www.mcs.drexel.edu/~crorres/ Archimedes/Lever/LeverIntro.html.*